Eat
Like a
Local

NEW YORK

BLOOMSBURY PUBLISHING
LONDON • OXFORD • NEW YORK • NEW DELHI • SYDNEY

Eat	14
Drink	106
Shop	118
Cook	130

Welcome to New York

Food is never just about food – it's access to an experience, a moment. To buy cheese, a baguette and olives and then lie back in the summertime grass of Manhattan's Central Park with thousands of other picnickers as the Metropolitan Opera performs a free public show is to steep in beauty and community and the thrill of something astonishing and grand – regardless of how good the cheese is.

To rise from a thoughtfully served, exquisitely prepared meal; to stroll through a late-spring farmers' market on the first Saturday that the tiny, sweet strawberries arrive; or to enter the cosy thrum of a Brooklyn beer hall on a snowy winter evening is to feel a part of something, to know a place a little better and to feel just a little more alive.

New York City has five boroughs – Manhattan, Brooklyn, Queens, the Bronx and Staten Island. Most visitors – like most New Yorkers, really – will become most familiar with the first three, if not the first two, or one. But all five have been shaped by the immigrants who over the centuries, the decades and the last few years have made this place home. New York is a celebration of cultures, creativity and diversity – which makes for some pretty incredible eating.

It isn't a simple or easy city, though – not in the way that simply beautiful places are. Rents are expensive, public transport is crowded and smelly, and competition is fierce for everything, from subway seats to table reservations. But, one comes to realise, that's part of its appeal. The challenges make the adventure that much sweeter.

Explore the City

Manhattan

Manhattan's **Downtown** encompasses the neighbourhoods long thought of as impossibly cool: the **West Village**, with its tiny, picture-perfect bistros; the younger, more eclectic **East Village**, with its strong multicultural options; the jumble of casual eating and shopping that is **Chinatown**; and **Soho** – once an artist's enclave and now a cobblestoned centre of high-end commerce and curated dining.

Chelsea, Gramercy and the **Flatiron** districts are home to the city's growing start-up scene and are a band of hip, young neighbourhoods with interesting restaurants, including Manhattan's pocket of south Asian cuisine.

Midtown, the band below Central Park, is where office workers commute to and tourists flock – for the Empire State Building, Rockefeller Center, the MoMA. It has long been considered a dining dead zone by locals, full of chain restaurants, office lunch spots and traps for tourists; but that makes its gems that much more delightful.

Uptown flanks Central Park: the tweedy, movie-ready **Upper West Side**, with its deli-based institutions and its less bookish, more ostentatious equivalent, the **Upper East Side**.

And still north of those is Upper Manhattan, which includes **Harlem** – with its increasingly serious dining scene – **Washington Heights** and **Inwood**. They're generally working-class, ethnically diverse neighbourhoods that are light on pretension and rich in potential, both in terms of culture and dining.

Brooklyn

Brooklyn is fast changing and hyper young – it's worth exploring the neighbourhoods constituting hipster headquarters: **Red Hook, Williamsburg** and **Greenpoint**, all hugging the water's edge, as well as the more interior **Crown Heights, Bushwick** and **Bedford-Stuyvesant.** They're neighbourhoods full of artisans, chefs and earnest and absurdist types. One can as easily stumble upon exquisite oysters as the offer of a straight-razor shave or bread made from hand-ground local grains, The flipside is brownstone Brooklyn. **Park Slope, Carroll Gardens, Brooklyn Heights** and **Fort Green** include immensely strollable blocks of architectural delights. The dining here is generally tamer, relaxed and family friendly. But there are happy exceptions, with young chefs vying to create something compelling and lasting – if not just a darn good cocktail.

Queens

Queens is one of the most diverse places on Earth. Residents hail from across Asia, Europe, Africa and South and Central America, making it home to some of the best and most unusual eating in New York. **Astoria** and **Jackson Heights** – laid out in easy-to-walk grids – are its most celebrated neighbourhoods and come up in nearly every conversation about where to find the best food and drink, whether it's a beer garden or home-style Greek, Pakistani, Colombian or Guyanese you're after.

Staten Island & The Bronx

These lesser-known boroughs are the city's most suburban and car-centric – **Staten Island** most of all. **The Bronx** is celebrated for having a strong immigrant culture that's represented in pockets of neighbourhoods and its largely informal but authentic restaurant scene. It's off the beaten path, but the richest rewards tend to be the hardest won.

Meet the Locals

Michelle Maisto

michellemaisto.com

Michelle Maisto is a food and technology writer in New York. She's the author of *The Gastronomy of Marriage: A Memoir of Food and Love* and has contributed to *The New York Times*, *Gourmet*, *Saveur* and a dozen tech sites.

Alex French

@FrenchAlexM

A freelance writer whose work has appeared in *GQ*, *New York Magazine*, *Details*, *The New York Times Magazine*, *The Los Angeles Times Magazine*, *Men's Journal*, *Grantland*, *This American Life* and numerous others.

Raquel Cepeda

djalirancher.com

A native New Yorker of Dominican parentage who currently works as an author, documentary filmmaker and cultural activist. She has written about varied subjects including music, culture, race and identity for publications such as *People*, *The New York Times* and *Time Out New York*.

Alana Hoye Barnaba

ahoynewyorkfoodtours.com

Owner of Ahoy New York Food Tours, an independent company offering food tours of Chinatown and Little Italy. She has formed solid relationships with the local shops and restaurants and considers this part of the city her second home.

Olivia & Jennie

@hungrygrls

The brains behind Hungrygrls, an Instagram account dedicated to all things food – from daily eats to the most coveted cuisines. Olivia and Jennie use captions, photography, food staging and as much humour as possible to shine a positive and engaging light on the (often overlooked) specific relationship that women and girls have with food.

Karl Wilder

secretfoodtours.com

A food-loving globetrotter who has worked in Italy, the Dominican Republic and Paris. Combining his passion for travel and eating, Karl currently works for Secret Food Tours in New York, where he helps runs gastronomical tours of Greenwich Village.

Laura Ferrara

@lauraferraranyc

A New York-based stylist and fashion editor who has worked with magazines such as *Allure* and *Glamour*. She also runs a certified organic orchard and cidery in Hudson Valley.

Vinh Nguyen

eatdrinkvinh.com

Restaurateur, chef and seafood expert, Vinh opened (the now defunct) Silent H in Williamsburg in 2005, kicking off the still-thriving *bahn mi* craze in New York City.

Marisel Salazar

mariselsalazar.com / @BreadButterNYC

A food and travel writer whose work has appeared on Tasting Table, Eater and Melting Butter. She works extensively with New York restaurants and has produced bespoke culinary events with James Beard award-winning, Michelin-starred and up-and-coming chefs across the US.

Roberto Serrini

robertoserrini.com

A travel writer who has been eating his way through this world since he was a teenager. Born and raised in NYC, he uses Gotham to jump off to remote parts of the world as a writer for *Get Lost* magazine. He is also a filmmaker who has created a handful of travel and food shows like *Make Me a Sandwich* (mmas.tv) where he asks his favourite chefs to make him their favourite sandwiches.

BRUNCH

Brunch, of course, sounds like a merger of breakfast and lunch – a gigantic meal! – but what it is more exactly is an offering of both sweet and savoury options.

Say you wake late, with a taste for something savoury – sausage and eggs, maybe, or a pork chop and waffles. But your travel companion still has a taste for breakfast – for something maple syrup doused, or a maybe a house-made granola with yoghurt and fruit. The answer? Brunch!

And still happier news: While brunch was traditionally relegated to the weekends, it's increasingly finding a weekday following, particularly in student- and hotel-heavy neighbourhoods.

How to identify a great brunch spot? There are 8.5 million people in this city – if a place is good, a line is a sure sign of that. Long lines don't form where the food is careless or quick. For what is likely your first meal of the day – possibly after a boozy, late night – brunch fare should coddle, soothe and revive as needed. Choose a place where someone has put serious care into the menu, with house-made savoury biscuits, slow-cooked polentas or stews, thick-cut French toast with tempting toppings and bacon with a pedigree.

The ideal is a combination of a great space, great staff, great food and great coffee. (Some might add: a killer Bloody Mary.) Many folks may settle for just two of those, but don't compromise on the coffee. If a restaurant takes pride in it, chances are they'll mention their roasting partners somewhere on the menu or near the coffee machine – which, like a clean restroom, is a good sign that attention is being paid to the details.

See also Gallow Green (page 89)

① Clinton St. Baking Company

Recommended by Alana Hoye Barnaba

"The best pancakes in New York City"—*AHB*

The husband-and-wife team behind the Clinton St. Baking Company opened their shop in 2001 with a single mission: to make the best baked goods in the city. Mission accomplished? Who knows – it's Clinton St.'s pancakes that this city is obsessed with. The queue, however, is as legendary as the pancakes, so consider the free app NoWait – it'll let you add your name to the queue if you're within a mile of the restaurant.

4 Clinton Street, East Village MN 10002
clintonstreetbaking.com • +1 6466026263
Open 7 days • $$$

② Café Mogador

Recommended by Raquel Cepeda

"I most often order the Middle Eastern breakfast with Turkish coffee. It's also my favourite place for work meetings"—*RC*

133 Wythe Avenue, Williamsburg BK 11249
(see website for other locations)
cafemogador.com • +1 7184869222
Open 7 days • $$$$

③ De Maria

Recommended by Laura Ferrara

"I do all-day breakfast at De Maria rather than brunch. It's a chic café at the edge of Nolita serving colourful salads and grain bowls from chef Camille Becerra"—*LF*

19 Kenmare Street, Nolita MN 10012
demarianyc.com • +1 2129663058
Open 7 days • $$$$

④ Tim Ho Wan

Recommended by Michelle Maisto

"Tim Ho Wan defies nearly every old dim sum trope. It's in the East Village, not Chinatown; it's done away with the rolling trolleys; and seriously everything on the menu is sensational. You will spend the next week replaying your first bite into the *char siu bao* (barbecue pork bun). The wait, though, is epic. Once you've given them your name and number, turn the corner down East 10th Street and hole up at City of Saints coffee roasters (page 115) – or grab a coffee (it's excellent) and set off on a two hour stroll"—*MM*

85 4th Avenue, East Village MN 10003
timhowanusa.com • +1 2122282800
Open 7 days • $$$$

⑤ El Malecon

Recommended by Kàrl Wilder

"No pricey avocado toast – just get a wholewheat tostada and some sliced avocado, mash with your fork, add some salt and spread. Delicious. With some poached eggs and a side of beans you get a filling and nutritious breakfast"—*KW*

764 Amsterdam Avenue, Upper West Side MN 10025
(see website for other locations)
maleconrestaurants.com • +1 2128645648
Open 7 days • $$$$

⑥ Selamat Pagi

Recommended by Marisel Salazar

"Balinese-inspired fare in a tropical environment"—*MS*

Selamat pagi means "good morning" in Indonesian. And certainly, this place feels like a wake-up call: one meal – with its bright, fragrant herbs, kick of spice, balance of tart and sweet, and plenty of vegetarian and vegan options – and you'll be wondering how there could possibly be so few Balinese restaurants in your life.

152 Driggs Avenue, Greenpoint BK 11222
selamatpagibrooklyn.com • +1 7187014333
Open 7 days, brunch served Saturday and Sunday • $$$$

BAGELS

In New York City, bagels are boiled in water and then baked, making for a glossy, crackly crust and a wonderfully squishy interior. An appropriately crackly-meets-squishy bagel could never be mistaken for bread.

Bagels are typically eaten for breakfast or brunch – or a weekend lunch, if you care to stack on the sandwich fillings. Toasting is for day-old bagels. Eat a fresh bagel as is, with a *schmear* (as the locals say) of cream cheese. Or gild that lily and add lox (smoked salmon cured in a salt-sugar rub), red onion, capers and maybe avocado. Or go the full-tilt bacon-egg-and-cheese route. There are no wrong answers. The crusty exterior – look for the gloss – of a fresh bagel will yield for a moment against the tug of sturdy front teeth, but give way before the sandwich threatens to fall apart. (With a day-old bagel, *fuhgettaboutit*.)

Bagels are not bank accounts: Bigger is not better. Bigger gets the ratio all wrong. Bigger is fluffy instead of squishy. Take a tip from Montreal, where bagels are smaller, denser and – because honey is added to the boiling-water – sweeter. The hole also tends be bigger, making them easy to spot.

New York now has a handful of Montreal-style bagel shops; if you find yourself near one, great. If not, zero worries. Locals don't travel more than ten blocks out of their way for a better bagel. Most neighbourhoods have numerous bagel shops. Take a look around, choose the one with smaller bagels, load it up, find a coffee and a copy of *The New York Times*, and know you're doing it right.

See also Zabar's (page 124)

⑦ Russ & Daughters

Recommended by Vinh Nguyen

"Great for bagels and smoked delectables"—*VN*

Russ & Daughters is a Jewish deli and a New York institution – not because it's been serving herring, bagels, salad platters and baked goods for 100-plus years, but because it's been setting the standard for that long. (Fun fact: When the progressive Joel Russ made his three daughters full partners in 1935, and changed the name of the shop to reflect that, it became the first shop in the United States with "& Daughters" in its name.)

179 East Houston Street, Lower East Side MN 10002
russanddaughterscafe.com • +1 2124754880
Open 7 days • $$$$

(8) Bagel Hole

Recommended by Michelle Maisto

"Bagel Hole is a rather fitting description of the shop itself – an ugly little space with old refrigerators filled with unimpressive breakfast basics like butter and orange juice. It looks utterly temporary, but since 1985 they have been hand-rolling some of the city's best bagels, in eleven flavours. There's no toaster, it's cash only and the coffee's terrible, but the bagels are a bite of heaven with the house-made lox spread"—*MM*

400 7th Avenue, Park Slope BK 11215
bagelhole.net • +1 7187884014
Open 7 days • $$$$

(9) Brooklyn Bagel & Coffee Company

Recommended by Roberto Serrini

"Brooklyn Bagel (which ironically is not in Brooklyn but Queens) has a pretty damn good bagel, but it's the *schmear* (spread of cream cheese) that really makes this place pop. For my money the best is a dug-out poppy with some tofu veggie in one side and white fish on the other"—*RS*

35–05 Broadway, Astoria QN 11106
(see website for other locations)
bkbagel.com • +1 7182040141
Open 7 days • $$$$

⑩ Black Seed Bagels

Recommended by Laura Ferrara, Vinh Nguyen, Olivia & Jennie

"Black Seed is a great spot when you're in need of some carbs. They serve Montreal-style bagels, which are smaller, thinner, sweeter and denser than NYC bagels, and baked in a wood-fired oven. I love how perfectly cooked they are – not chewy, with a really nice consistency"—*LF*

"Small and insanely satisfying"—*O&J*

176 1st Avenue, East Village MN 10009
(see website for other locations)
blackseedbagels.com • +1 6464845718
Open 7 days • $$$$

SANDWICHES

This lunchtime hero comes in about as many incarnations as the people who enjoy it.

You can go the Jewish deli route (pastrami, corned beef, mustard, pickles); grab a Vietnamese *banh mi* (pickled vegetables, pork pâté, coriander); hunt down a lobster roll (succulent, buttery summertime); opt for Middle Eastern (try stuffing French fries inside your falafel sandwich); or stick with classic New York, which is to say, the hero – or submarine sandwich – itself.

A classic hero brings together salty meats like ham or salami, a mild smooth cheese such as provolone or mozzarella, a bit of crunch in the form of lettuce or salad, and a vinegar element, to counterbalance the salty, fatty meat (think spicy peppers or lightly pickled vegetables).

Nearly every corner deli, or *bodega* (places that sell everything one might run to the store for at 11pm) has a deli counter serving sandwiches. Avoid these. Instead, go somewhere focused solely on food.

House-made mozzarella, high quality meats, good pickled options and fresh Italian bread (squishy on the inside, not fluffy) that can hug a row of meatballs without losing its integrity are all good signs.

Whatever kind of sandwich you decide on, consider the following: Is there a menu board making your mouth water? Are the ingredients fresh? Are you thinking you couldn't possibly eat the whole thing? Then you may be in the right place.

See also Saigon Vietnamese Sandwich Deli (page 101)

⑪ Harry and Ida's

Recommended by Roberto Serrini

"There is only one sandwich that can be called king in NYC: Will Horowitz's grandpa's pastrami sandwich at his speciality shop Harry and Ida's in the East Village. Pastrami so tender he cuts it with the back of a knife, Japanese buttermilk fermented pickles, harissa and Gulden's mustard spread. Google it. Watch the video. Cover your keyboard with a towel for you will drool"—*RS*

189 Avenue A, East Village MN 10009
(see website for other locations)
harryandidas.com • +1 6468640967
Open 7 days • $$$$

12 Oasis

Recommended by Alex French

"Oasis, the little falafel shop tucked behind the entrance to the L-train on Bedford Street in Williamsburg, is my favourite place to eat a sandwich. Superb people-watching meets perfect, pillowy paddies of deep-fried chickpea, fresh and hot pita, white sauce and little Middle Eastern pickles that are confoundingly delicious"—AF

161 North 7th Street, Williamsburg BK 11211
+1 7182187607
Open 7 days • $$$

- -

13 DeFonte's

Recommended by Michelle Maisto

"The Valentino Special (named after a neighbourhood firefighter who died in the line of duty) is probably the only aubergine (eggplant) Parmesan I've ever liked – and certainly the only one I've ever loved. By some magic, the fried aubergine is squishy and resilient, as opposed to mushy and messy, and a perfect complement to the milky, fresh-made mozzarella"—MM

379 Columbia Street, Red Hook BK 11231
+1 7186258052
Closed Sunday • $$$

- -

14 V-Nam Café

Recommended by Raquel Cepeda

"Great Vietnamese *banh mi*. I like to order them with extra jalapeño peppers" —RC

20 1st Avenue, Lower East Side MN 10003
vnamcafe.com • +1 2127806020
Open 7 days • $$$

⑮ A&S Fine Foods

Recommended by Laura Ferrara

"An authentic neighbourhood deli and pork store in the heart of Brooklyn, where gentrification hasn't yet hit. Unlike some of the imposter eateries that have taken the DNA from the original Italian-American *salumeria* and become hipster destinations in the Lower East Side, I always like to go to the original because that's where true New York characters hang out"—*LF*

361 Avenue X, Gravesend BK 11223
asporkstoreavex.com • +1 7183363373
Open 7 days • $$$

DOUGHNUTS & PASTRIES

New York has a strong bakery tradition and there are a handful of beloved shops that have been serving the same *cannoli*, *babka* and *baklava* recipes for generations, in storefronts that have changed just as little. These tend to exist in neighbourhoods where an ethnic old guard – the Italians in Carroll Gardens, say, or the Russians in Brighton Beach – has yet to fully surrender to gentrification. And then there are the few shops, like Veniero's (page 30), standing their ground by some miracle of real estate.

Set against those delicious, old-school traditions are the bakery trends, which tend to be as gloriously excessive as the 80s were to Wall Street. While the noughties saw the rise of the cupcake, this is the decade of the doughnut.

The ubiquitous orange-pink-and-brown doughnut brand New Yorkers grew up with is now a preservative-filled joke in a landscape of young brands competing to out-awesome each other with organic, house-made ingredients, freshness and incredible creativity.

Not a doughnut person? The city is now also sprinkled with hybrid pastries, such as the cronut (Dominique Ansel's croissant-doughnut, page 32) and cake truffles (Milk Bar's cake balls rolled in cake crumbs, page 93). Whatever your sugar-meets-butter format of choice, make sure it was baked within the last 24 hours and from ingredients you wouldn't be horrified to feed a baby.

Let it be known (to the guilty sorts among us) that there is no wrong time for a doughnut, or its ilk. New Yorkers eat desserts for breakfast, for snacks, for dessert, on dates. And we compete with them in offices ("Now, *these* are the best [insert food item] in New York!"). Your body may not forgive you if you eat a sweet treat for breakfast every day, but no one else will blink an eye.

⑯ Peter Pan Donuts

Recommended by Vinh Nguyen

"The best doughnuts, plus I like how the place is just timeless"—*VN*

Peter Pan Donuts is a 60-something-year-old, no-frills doughnut diner in Greenpoint, Brooklyn, where the staff still wear I Love Lucy-esque uniforms. Doughnuts are priced under $2, nothing is fancy and everything's terrific.

727 Manhattan Avenue, Greenpoint BK 11222
peterpandonuts.com • +1 7183893676
Open 7 days • $$$$

⑰ Veniero's

Recommended by Roberto Serrini

"Veniero's on 11th has been baking since 1894 and going there is like tasting history. Their classic Italian almond cake is one of those things that tastes like nothing else and it's something I crave from time to time"—*RS*

342 East 11th Street, East Village MN 10003
venierosnewyork.com • +1 2126747070
Open 7 days • $$$$

18 · Villabate Alba

Recommended by Laura Ferrara

"For pastries I go to Villabate Alba, which is an Italian-American bakery at its best. During the holidays, you can get a marzipan nativity set as well as Easter bread and traditional southern Italian pastries. With Little Italy long gone places like this are the last fragments of authenticity in a gentrifying New York City. A scene from Saturday Night Fever was shot near here"—*LF*

7001 18th Avenue, Bensonhurst BK 11204
villabate.com • +1 7183318430
Open 7 days • $$$$

19 · Molly's Cupcakes

Recommended by Raquel Cepeda

"Molly's Cupcakes on Bleecker are crack. My absolute favourite are the centre-filled cake batter cupcakes. If I'm going to have a cheat day, I might as well go balls-to-the-wall"—*RC*

228 Bleecker Street, West Village MN 10014
mollyscupcakes.com • +1 2124142253
Open 7 days • $$$$

20 · Dominique Ansel Bakery

Alana Hoye Barnaba

"It's the home of the cronut (croissant-doughnut) but it has a ton more creative and delicious desserts"—*AHB*

189 Spring Street, Soho MN 10012
dominiqueansel.com • +1 2122192773
Open 7 days • $$$$

21 Doughnut Plant

Recommended by Michelle Maisto

"Doughnut Plant started in the basement of a Lower East Side tenement, with Mark Isreal, a third-generation doughnut maker, experimenting with his grandfather's recipe. He settled into recipes featuring local, seasonal ingredients and glazes, and later spent years developing the perfect cake doughnut. After that came variations including a filled, square doughnut (with a hole!); savoury doughpods; and special flavours for special occasions – like a Candy Corn doughnut filled with house-made corn pudding and a Mardi Gras King Cake doughnut. How to choose? That's the beauty – you can't go wrong"—*MM*

379 Grand Street, Lower East Side MN 10002
(see website for other locations)
doughnutplant.com • +1 2125053700
Open 7 days • $$$$

CHINATOWN

Brooklyn has a thriving Chinatown, and the Chinatown in Queens is widely thought to be the most authentic and to have the best food. But the one in lower Manhattan is, without a doubt, considered New York's Chinatown.

Manhattan's Chinatown is growing by the day and, with a younger generation asserting itself, shedding its old caricature for something more interesting. Ramen and chicken and waffles can now be found, but so can plenty of the classics, like roasted duck in steamed buns and lemongrass-steamed whole fish.

Grazing and walking may be the best way to discover one's own Chinatown. Lead with your curiosity and you can't get it wrong. Head down Canal from Broadway and zigzag the streets. Buy fruit from the street carts (lychee and longan are easy to peel as you go – or a good excuse to sit and people-watch). Stop in bakeries for slices of sponge cake, yeasty-sweet *bai-tang-gou* (think Rice Krispies treats, if they were actually made with steamed rice) and *dan-ta*, little muffin-sized custard pies. And if you encounter a sidewalk line, be brave and ask questions – there's often something delicious at the front of it.

When you're ready to sit, eat where you see Chinese people eating. Don't be afraid to share a large table. Glance around at what's on other tables (often a better way to order than the menu). And skip dessert.

Instead, head out in search of one of the new dessert or ice cream shops that are a distinctive mark of Chinatown's second generation (page 92). Flavours tend to be a mash-up of traditional Chinese (red bean, condensed milk, black sesame) and 80s childhood (Lucky Charms marshmallows, crushed Nutterbutters), making for a truly authentic, and delicious, taste of a place and time.

22 Fried Dumpling

Recommended by Laura Ferrara

"An unassuming spot tucked away deep in Chinatown on Mosco Street, near Columbus Park. Authentic Chinatown dumplings at 5 for $1, who can beat that deal?"—*LF*

106 Mosco Street, Chinatown MN 10013
+1 2126931060
Open 7 days • $$$$

. . . .

23 Thai Son

Recommended by Raquel Cepeda

"A no-frills Vietnamese spot on an unassuming block that I like to slip away to on those days when I'm not thinking about calories"—*RC*

89 Baxter Street, Chinatown MN 10013
+1 2127322822
Open 7 days • $$$$

. . . .

24 New World Mall

Recommended by Roberto Serrini

"Head out to Flushing, Queens on the 7-train where the REAL Chinatown is, go to the bottom of the New World Mall, and try to navigate the extensive and completely Chinese food court. You will feel like you are in Shanghai"—*RS*

136–20 Roosevelt Avenue, Flushing QN 11354
+1 7183530551
Closed Saturday and Sunday • $$$$

25 Nom Wah Tea Parlor

*Recommended by Alana Hoye
Barnaba, Roberto Serrini*

"The oldest dim sum parlour in
Chinatown. All their absolutely
delicious dim sum is made to order"
—AHB

"It's on the most cinematic alley in
all of Chinatown. Dim sum to die
for"—RS

*13 Doyers Street,
Chinatown MN 10013
(see website for other locations)
nomwah.com
Open 7 days • $$$$*

㉖ Xi'an Famous Foods

Recommended by Marisel Salazar

"The cumin lamb noodles and burger are the most popular items"—*MS*

Though it now has twelve branches, Xi'an Famous Foods' success comes from staying true to its beginnings in a Queens basement food stall, serving inexpensive, authentic food from Xi'an (pronounced *she-on*), China. Don't miss the hand-pulled noodles.

45 Bayard Street, Chinatown MN 10013
(see website for other locations)
xianfoods.com
Open 7 days • $$$

27 Kopitiam

Recommended by Marisel Salazar

"This teeny blue Chinatown café adorned with lucky cats and a laughing Buddha is modelled after the coffee shops in Malaysia"—*MS*

In Malaysia, *kopitiam* is generic term for the type of snack-centred coffee shop where customers sip and while away a day. That won't work at the four-seat Kopitiam, which is fiercely loved for both its intensely savoury dishes (think fermented shrimp paste and anchovies) and its outstanding house-made sweets. (Souvenir tip: It's well worth bringing home a jar of the proprietress' homemade coconut jam.)

51B Canal Street, Chinatown MN 10002
+1 6468947081
Closed Monday • $$$$

28 Fei Long Market Food Court

Recommended by Michelle Maisto

"'Food court' may be the two least appetising words – until you enter the chaos of the Fei Long Market in Brooklyn's Chinatown. Leading up to the entrance of the large Asian grocery store is a room ringed by stalls of inexpensive foods of varying quality – an exciting prospect for a certain personality. There are places with hand-pulled noodles, stir-fries, spit-roasted duck, and soups made on the spot with ingredients you point out. My favourite is the first stall on the left, where through the glass window you can watch the cooks hand-pleating every manner of *xiao long bao* (soup dumplings)"—*MM*

6301 8th Avenue, Sunset Park BK 11220
Open 7 days • $$$$

JAPANESE

This town is packed with mediocre, so-called Japanese restaurants. But a few quick dos and don'ts can help to sift through the options...

Don't eat anywhere with the words Teriyaki, Sushi, Tokyo, Ninja or Wasabi in the title. *Don't* eat anywhere that advertises "All You Can Eat" or "50% Off". And *don't* even crack the front door of any place that offers the cuisines of more than one Asian country (Japanese and Chinese, say).

Do take heart if actual Japanese people are running the restaurant and/or preparing the food.

Do count your blessings if you walk into a ramen restaurant and the scent of a long-cooking broth envelops you and keeps you whimpering until a bowl is set before you.

If it's sushi you're after, *do* take a seat at the bar if the restaurant smells lightly of seawater, but not of fish (fresh fish doesn't smell fishy) and has a sushi roll menu that's no more than a page long.

As for *izakaya* restaurants – which serve small plates of Japan's (elevated) equivalent of bar food – look for a cosy atmosphere, buzzing tables passing delicious-looking dishes, and a good sake list.

Winning spots are dotted around the city. But walk the blocks of East 9th Street and Saint Mark's Place (the equivalent of East 8th Street) between 2nd and 3rd Avenues, if you want to throw a dart that's unlikely to miss the mark.

29 Mama Sushi

Recommended by Raquel Cepeda

"This is my favourite restaurant as they fuse Japanese and Dominican food in an unexpected and yet harmonious way. I love how they re-envision traditional Dominican staples such as *maduros* (fried ripe plantains) and *queso frito* (fried cheese) as sushi rolls"—*RC*

3569 Broadway Avenue, Harlem MN 10033
(see website for other locations)
mamasushi.com • +1 6466827879
Open 7 days • $$$$

. . . .

30 Hasaki

Recommended by Laura Ferrara

"I have been going here for twenty years and it's still one of my favourite places for Japanese food. I love this spot, it's unassuming – with a discreet below-ground storefront in the East Village – and perfectly delicious"—*LF*

210 East 9th Street, East Village MN 10003
hasakinyc.com • +1 2124733327
Open 7 days • $$$$

. . . .

31 Kyo Ya

Recommended by Vinh Nguyen

"My family once took me to Kyo Ya and I still refer people here for amazing Japanese fare. Start with some sushi but finish with the crab fried rice"—*VN*

94 East 7th Street, East Village MN 10009
+1 2129824140
Open 7 days • $$$$

32 Omen Azen

Recommended by Laura Ferrara

"I love the fact that at this restaurant some of the most interesting people in the world could be seated next to you but they always have a table available. I like the unpretentious, serene vibe. The food is always delicious and I particularly love their avocado salad" —*LF*

113 Thompson Street, Soho MN 10012
omen-azen.com • +1 2129258923
Open 7 days • $$$$

33 Karasu

Recommended by Vinh Nguyen

"A gem hidden behind Walter Foods.
The menu is small but so good and,
when eaten alongside a few of their
drinks, you feel like you are in a little
secret spot in Nakameguro, Tokyo"
—VN

166 Dekalb Avenue,
Fort Greene BK 11217
karasubk.com • +1 3472234811
Open 7 days • $$$$

PIZZA

Scientists need a name for the umami pleasure explosion that is the first bite from a half-folded, piping-hot slice of paper-plate-staining pizza; the moment when the front teeth gingerly clip the isosceles, sending a small cheese avalanche flowing and the brain and the mouth simultaneously registering softness and crunch, sweetness and salt.

Pizza slice prices follow subway ride prices – currently around $3 – but it's possible to find $1 slices in the type of Midtown storefronts where the counter abuts the sidewalk. And in moments of great hunger or frigid cold or giddy drunkenness, those slices can be divine.

But in most other moments, when pizza is eaten as a meal, rather than inhaled as a cure, go where pizza-making is treated as both an art and a science. Look for house-made mozzarella, hormone-free meats, seasonal toppings and maybe an inflexible *No Substitutions* policy (which suggests an artist is at work).

That said, it's a rookie mistake to think a pizza is as good as its toppings. What makes a great pizza is high quality cheese, sauce and dough, combined at the right ratio and cooked to perfection by people who understand their oven. Where there are toppings, they should be as fresh and considered as the rest of the pie. An easy giveaway is mushrooms: If they're round and nubby and clearly from a tin, keep moving.

But if you're greeted by the sight of a studied *pizzaiolo*, working at a slab of marble with a glass bowl of fresh mozzarellas and a licking fire in the brick oven behind him, sit down immediately.

See also Zero Otto Nove (page 55)

㉞ Babbalucci

Recommended by Karl Wilder

"All I can say is wow. This eatery, opened by a father and son, is known for their killer pizza with a light, crisp crust and fresh mozzarella. The kitchen is also a force to be reckoned with – some incredible pastas come forth. Get everything and share with a group of friends"—*KW*

331 Lenox Avenue, Harlem MN 10027
babbalucci.com • +1 6469186572
Open 7 days • $$$$

35 Saraghina

Recommended by Laura Ferrara

"Housed in an old ground-floor building, Saraghina reminds me of growing up in Brooklyn and my grandma's backyard. Eating outside amongst the vines growing in the garden feels nostalgic and homey, but with an edge and a fun Brooklyn crowd"—*LF*

435 Halsey Street,
Bedford-Stuyvesant BK 11233
saraghinabrooklyn.com
+1 7185740010
Open 7 days • $$$$

㊱ Ribalta

Recommended by Roberto Serrini

"Let's get specific. For *Neapolitan style*, then it's Ribalta on 12th street, where master *pizzaiolo* Pasquale Cozzolino might belt a bit of opera out for you as he twirls your pie right from the bay of Naples"—*RS*

48 East 12th Street, Gramercy MN 10003
ribaltapizzarestaurant.com • +1 2127777781
Open 7 days • $$$$

37 Brooklyn Firefly

Recommended by Raquel Cepeda

"Beyond good, especially the square pies. Although, as a New York native, Brooklyn doesn't excite me any more, this spot inspires me to put my reservations on ice. I'm looking forward to seeing how their menu expands over time"—RC

7003 3rd Avenue, Bay Ridge BK 11209
thebrooklynfirefly.com • +1 7188335000
Closed Monday • $$$$

38 Lucali's

Recommended by Roberto Serrini

"For a real Italian thin crust you have to go to Carroll Gardens and wait in line at Lucali's. I won't even try to explain how good it is because using words would just be insulting"—RS

575 Henry Street, Red Hook BK 11231
lucali.com • +1 7188584086
Closed Tuesday • $$$$

39 Stromboli Pizza

Recommended by Roberto Serrini

"Best NYC slice, hands down, is Stromboli on Saint Marks. Has been the best for the last 23 years"—RS

83 Saint Marks Place, Gramercy MN 10003
strombolipizzeria.com • +1 2126733691
Open 7 days • $$$$

⑩ Giuseppina's Brick Oven Pizza

Recommended by Michelle Maisto

"Giuseppina's in Greenwood is the sister restaurant to the famous Lucali's in Carroll Gardens (opposite). Or rather, the brother restaurant, as the *pizzaiolo* holding forth in a crisp white t-shirt, silhouetted by the wood-fed oven behind him, is Chris Iacono, brother of Lucali's owner Mark Iacono. Giuseppina's serves only pizza, calzones and beverages. But who cares about a green salad when the pizza – never mushy at the centre, and with a crust that shatters more than tears – is so achingly good. It's candlelit and still family friendly"—*MM*

691 6th Avenue, Greenwood BK 11215
+1 7184995052
Closed Tuesday • $$$$

ITALIAN

Whether stepping out of the snow for a bowl of oxtail ragu or escaping a steamy summer sidewalk for a three-course meal and cold glass of Verdicchio, there's Italian food for every desire and price point.

There's also a lot of mediocre Italian food, especially where it slips into Italian-American cuisine. The difference between the two? Broadly speaking, Italian-American cuisine is more saucy and (arguably) less elegant. Whereas an Italian restaurant nodding at a region of Italy is more likely to offer dishes with few ingredients, but with each one treated as a star.

So take a look at the menu. There shouldn't be too many options. For example, eight pastas, or *primi*, is about right. If it reads like a diner menu, or offers dishes across multiple ethnicities, don't do it. And if there's a list of macaroni shapes and a list of sauces to mix and match on your whim, keep moving. (That pesto, say, is so often paired with orecchiette, is intentional; there's a balance between pasta heft and function and the weight or delicacy of a sauce that a proper chef will respect.)

Also, is the meat local or hormone-free? Does the restaurant mention working with nearby farms? Are the vegetable dishes seasonal? Are any of the pastas homemade? And is there a warning that a particular dish, perhaps the risotto, requires some patience? These are good signs.

And of course, take a look around. The clichés about the warmth of Italians is rooted in something very real. The restaurant should be a space you want to enjoy a glass of wine in and relax into; where people look like they're happy with their choices; and – a good sign of a small thing done well – where diners are eagerly tucking into the bread basket, versus turning to it in desperation.

41 Zero Otto Nove

Recommended by Raquel Cepeda

"There's an abundance of great Italian eateries in New York but, after giving it serious thought, Zero Otto Nove on Arthur Avenue in the Boogie Down Bronx is my absolute favourite. Their brick oven pizza is the second best I've tasted in the world and the ambience is just chill" —*RC*

2357 Arthur Avenue, Belmont BX 10458
(see website for other locations)
089bronx.com • +1 7182201027
Closed Monday • $$$$

42 Bar Primi

Recommended by Olivia & Jennie

"It's perfect for every occasion"—*O&J*

Bar Primi is casual but elegant; home-style but professional. It's like going to eat at your Italian grandmother's house – if your grandmother were a sensational chef who insisted on organic eggs and non-GM semolina, her home and tableware and plated dishes were all magazine-ready, and she kept a killer wine cellar.

325 Bowery, Gramercy MN 10003
barprimi.com • +1 2122209100
Open 7 days • $$$$

43 Via Carota

Recommended by Laura Ferrara

"At Via Carota there's always a warm and lively feeling, like you just stepped into a *trattoria* in Italy. Jody Williams, the owner and chef, is always making sure the customers are having the best meal and a wonderful evening, just like you'd find at the most enjoyable places in Italy"—*LF*

51 Grove Street, West Village MN 10014
viacarota.com
Open 7 days • $$$$

44 I Sodi

Recommended by Laura Ferrara

"This intimate restaurant is not pretentious; it simply offers great Italian food in a small place with huge ambience. Rita Sodi, the owner and chef, is always around and making sure the customers are having a good time"—*LF*

105 Christopher Street, West Village MN 10014
isodinyc.com • +1 2124145774
Open 7 days • $$$$

45 Hearth

Recommended by Roberto Serrini

"Oddly enough, there's a little American bistro called Hearth in the Village that has an off-menu *Cacio e Pepe* (pasta with pecorino cheese and black pepper) that makes me cry. Pro's tip: Sit at the back bar in the kitchen and watch the magic happen; somehow the food tastes even better"—*RS*

403 East 12th Street, East Village MN 10009
restauranthearth.com • +1 6466021300
Open 7 days • $$$$

BURGERS

If you're eating meat, make it good meat. The beef in your New York burger should come from cows that were hormone-free, sustainably raised, grass-fed and ideally local. These details matter and any restaurant worth eating at will mention them on its menu. It's worth bearing in mind that, while it's fun to find a little-known spot, when a place is known for its burger that means it's cooking hundreds of them a day and its staff will have acquired an expertise that's meaningful.

That settled, it's a matter of: What kind of burger person are you? Do you like a small, backyard-style beauty that's an even ratio of beef to bun, outfitted with little more than lettuce, tomato and cheese, and can be held in one hand? Or, do you go in for a tall, pub-style, charred-on-the-outside, red-on-the-inside burger you have to wrestle with two hands (or, more civilly, with a knife and fork)?

Backyard-style tends to be what you find at places that crank out burgers all day (no judgement there) and perhaps serve them wrapped in paper, rather than plated (the ubiquitous Shake Shack, page 62, is the best example of this).

But if you sit down at a proper restaurant with non-burger main course options, or sidle up to a nice bar and order a beer while you wait to be served a meal – a burger served on a plate with fries and maybe some kind of salad – it's very likely a pub-style burger you'll be served. And in those instances, the topping options also tend to be more creative.

Should you pile on the toppings? Go for that secret sauce? Have it medium-well done or rare? These are personal decisions. You do as you see fit, friend.

46 Burger Joint

Recommended by Michelle Maisto

"As hotel amenities go, Burger Joint – a 'secret' restaurant behind a curtain in the lobby of Le Parker Meridien hotel – is hard to beat. And really, it's a kindness to everyone in Midtown after dark. It's a small, graffitied room that's all about excellence through precision and simplicity: a special recipe minced in-house every day; a five-ounce burger; a toasted Arnold potato bun; white Cheddar and Colby cheeses; and the classic backyard fixings. Hospitality genius"—*MM*

Le Parker Meridien, 119 West 56th Street, Midtown MN 10019
burgerjointny.com • +1 2127087414
Open 7 days • $$$

⁴⁷ The Spotted Pig

Recommended by Laura Ferrara

"I think April Bloomfield is one of the most talented chefs in New York City. The Spotted Pig has a beautiful interior and exterior, housed in an endearing West Village corner building. The burger here has a well-deserved great reputation. It comes with Roquefort cheese (which I don't usually like), it's always perfectly cooked and it's delicious with shoestring French fries"—*LF*

314 West 11th Street,
West Village MN 10014
thespottedpig.com • +1 2126200393
Open 7 days • $$$$

48 Shake Shack

Recommended by Michelle Maisto

"Chef Danny Meyer's ubiquitous Shake Shack chain got its start as a cart on the south-east corner of Madison Square Park. That cart has since been upgraded to a kiosk selling roadside stand-style shakes, hot dogs and straightforward burgers with standard toppings on potato buns. They're the in-a-rush, walking-by-the-park go-to meal. For pre-meditated visits, there's an online webcam where potential guests can check on the queue"—MM

Madison Avenue & East 23rd Street, Flatiron MN 10010
(see website for other locations)
shakeshack.com • +1 2128896600
Open 7 days • $$$$

49 J.G. Melon

Recommended by Vinh Nguyen

"I like smaller burgers – no frills, no fuss. I love an old-school burger from J.G. Melon"—VN

There are now three locations of J.G. Melon, which first opened in 1972 and more or less instantly became famous for its cheeseburger: seven and a quarter ounces of a special beef blend (the exact recipe is a secret), griddle cooked, wrapped in melting American cheese and served with pickles and thinly sliced onion on a soft, toasted bun.

89 MacDougal Street, Flatiron MN 10012
(see website for other locations)
jgmelonnyc.com • +1 2124600900
Open 7 days • $$$$

50 Springbone

Recommended by Karl Wilder

"To my mind, this is the one place to go for burgers. Instead of a bun, the grass-fed meat is served on a lightly grilled Portobello mushroom with sautéed onions. Beefy heaven"—*KW*

90 West 3rd Street, Soho MN 10012
springbone.com • +1 6463689192
Open 7 days • $$$$

51 Brindle Room

Recommended by Roberto Serrini

"Brindle Room. Period. No questions. Best burger in the world. Jeremy Spector was born from a patty years ago, and brought his magic to the East Village to make, bar none, the best burger in the world. This propriety blend, deckle-cut, seared in a cast-iron skillet burger topped with caramelised onions, Cheddar cheese and classic white bun will absolutely make you cry"—RS

277 East 10th Street, East Village MN 10009
brindleroom.com • +1 2125299702
Open 7 days • $$$$

52 Minetta Tavern

Recommended by Marisel Salazar

"Go for the famous Black Label Burger"—MS

A 1977 *New York Times* review made the burger at Minetta Tavern famous. The restaurant has since undergone a speakeasy-ish steakhouse makeover, but the burger remains as beloved as ever. Among the secrets to its success is the exclusive use of outstanding dry-aged beef.

113 MacDougal Street, Soho MN 10012
minettatavernny.com • +1 2124753850
Open 7 days • $$$$

53 ## Burger and Lobster

Recommended by Alana Hoye Barnaba

"The burger is juicy and topped with cheese and bacon. What more can you ask for?"—*AHB*

In addition to burgers in various sizes, lobsters dressed various ways and a *foie gras*/lobster/burger combination that your cardiologist would advise against, this UK import serves cocktails, mocktails and dessert.

39 West 19th Street, Flatiron MN 10011
burgerandlobster.com • +1 6468337532
Open 7 days • $$$$

LATIN

Latin food in Manhattan – whether from Spain, Mexico or South and Central America – tends to be the work of studied chefs, backed by investors and marketing teams. From tapas restaurants to Brazilian steakhouses and paella specialists, excellent restaurants with composed plates and exquisite ingredients are sprinkled around the island.

The *other* boroughs are where you go to find neighbourhood pockets representing a cuisine, with dishes (for the most part) prepared casually, the way they are in homes.

For Dominican, Colombian, Uruguayan, Peruvian, Ecuadorian or Mexican foods, there's no beating the stretch of Roosevelt Avenue between roughly 74th and 108th Streets, in Jackson Heights, Queens. You could spend a happy day strolling the streets of the most diverse neighbourhood on the planet and stuffing a bag with leftovers and snacks.

In Brooklyn, the northern end of Sunset Park has a bustling Mexican community. And during the summer weekends, the food truck scene ringing the Red Hook baseball fields (where the teams are mostly Latino men) make the games worth visiting, whether you're a ball fan or not.

On hot days, make sure to leave room (and scan the menu boards) for *paletas* (Mexican ice-pops in truly every conceivable flavour) and *cholados*, Colombia's over-the-top version of the shaved-ice dessert *halo-halo*.

54 El Economico

Recommended by Karl Wilder

"Like grandma makes, if you are lucky enough to have a Dominican grandmother. Where to begin? Crisp pork skin that's fried to a beautiful crackly texture, spiced roast chicken, plantains, rice and beans. A beautiful canon of delicious food and, as the name indicates, a bargain. Share everything – they have never made a small portion in their lives"—*KW*

5589 Broadway, Kingsbridge BX 10436
+1 7187964851
Open 7 days • $$$$

. . . .

55 La Nueva España

Recommended by Raquel Cepeda

"The best Dominican restaurant in New York City, with the most misleading name. I have been going there for a couple of decades now and still have no clue what the cuisine has to do with our former colonisers. They are known for their grilled chicken called *pollo a la parilla*. I suggest sharing a bunch of dishes on a night when there's karaoke (usually Fridays): it's loud and festive"—*RC*

606 West 207th Street, Inwood MN 10034
+1 2125670500
Open 7 days • $$$$

. . . .

56 Los Tacos No.1

Recommended by Vinh Nguyen

"Chelsea Market (a huge indoor food hall) is a great place to visit. Every time I'm there I get tacos from Los Tacos No.1 – simply the best tacos in NYC right now"—*VN*

Chelsea Market, 75 9th Avenue, Chelsea MN 10011
(see website for other locations)
lostacos1.com • +1 2122460343
Open 7 days • $$$$

57 Panca

Recommended by Raquel Cepeda

"I absolutely dig the fun atmosphere and ceviche at this Peruvian restaurant" —RC

True to the roots of Peruvian cuisine, Panca brings together high-end ingredients and influences from Spain, China, Japan, Italy and Africa. It has a curved wooden bar, perfect for sidling up to for a pisco sour (cocktails and nibbles are offered at reduced prices from 5pm to 7pm) and a menu of dishes meant to be shared family-style.

92 7th Avenue South, West Village MN 10014
pancany.com • +1 2124883900
Open 7 days • $$$$

58 ATLA

Recommended by Vinh Nguyen

"For really great modern Mexican food that highlights the culture's beautiful ingredients and flavours, sit at the bar at ATLA and try their crowd favourites!"—*VN*

372 Lafayette Street,
Nolita MN 10012
atlanyc.com
Open 7 days • $$$$

SOUTH ASIAN

The borough of Queens is said to be *the* most ethnically diverse urban area on the planet, with more languages spoken (167, by one count) than anywhere.

Its neighbourhood of Jackson Heights is home to Indian, Nepali and Pakistani communities, which makes for fantastic eating – and shopping. Take the E, F, M or R subway lines to the Roosevelt Avenue station, and you can spend the better part of a day walking the triangle of streets between Broadway, 37th Avenue and Roosevelt Avenue.

Between meals, you can shop for a sari, buy gold bangles, browse grocery store shelves and nibble at bakery sweets and street food. Even the neighbourhood's old namesake diner has transitioned over and now serves an all-day Indian buffet.

In Manhattan, head to Lexington Avenue between 26th and 29th Streets. In terms of volume, it's no Jackson Heights, but there are at least a dozen options between those blocks, from vegetarian south Indian fare to north Indian kebab places. Compared to the general home-style trend in Queens, this Manhattan stretch tends to be a touch more formal, with more mainstream, designed dining rooms and crisp, white tablecloths. The neighbourhood also has a few small speciality grocery stores that are well worth popping into, to see what you might find.

59 Hanoi House

Recommended by Vinh Nguyen

"Hanoi House is where you want to go. The queue to get a table can be long, but with chef John playing around with ingredients and flavour you can definitely expect some winning twists on Vietnamese staples"—*VN*

119 Saint Marks Place, East Village MN 10009
hanoihousenyc.com • +1 2129955010
Open 7 days • $$$$

60 **Pye Boat**

Recommended by Roberto Serrini

"This place is off the charts. Rich,
delicious broth, hand-pulled noodles
– like you're barefoot in Koh Pi Pi"
—RS

35–13 Broadway, Astoria QN 11106
+1 7186852329
Open 7 days • $$$$

61 Indochine

Recommended by Laura Ferrara

"Indochine is one of my old stomping grounds from the late 80s and early 90s in New York. I'll always love it"—*LF*

Indochine – with its stark, green palm-leaf wallpaper and French-Vietnamese colonialist vibe – opened in 1984 and is still, successfully, working its early Andy Warhol allure. For the theatre crowd, it serves a special menu from 5.30pm to 7pm.

430 Lafayette Street, East Village MN 10003
indochinenyc.com • +1 2125055111
Open 7 days • $$$$

62 # Pongal

Recommended by Michelle Maisto

"Pongal has a slim, lovely dining room, serves vegetarian dishes from southern India, and excels at *dosa* (enormous, crisp, funnel-like shells housing vegetarian fillings) and *uttapam* (thick pancake with toppings like coconut and coriander, or peppers and peas). I'm sure the *uttapam* is delicious, but I can never bring myself to not order a tornado-shaped *dosa*, with its small, misleadingly satisfying scoop of filling hidden inside. With a tall glass of cold beer, it's carb heaven"—MM

110 Lexington Avenue, Midtown MN 10016
newyorkpongal.com • +1 2126969458
Open 7 days • $$$$

63 # Patel Brothers

Recommended by Michelle Maisto

"Don't leave New York without a visit to Patel Brothers. It may be the world's most no-nonsense global grocery store, with everything from rare produce to fresh-made *pani puri* (puffed, crisp bread filled with potato and chutney) and frozen *kulfi* from Rajbhog – an ice cream and sweet shop down the street"
—MM

37–27 74th Street, Jackson Heights QN 11372
(see website for other locations)
patelbros.com • +1 7188983445
Open 7 days • $$$$

64 # Kismat

Recommended by Raquel Cepeda

"Unassuming, off the beaten path and laid back. The vegetable korma is just the right amount of sweet; it's subtle, and amazing when paired with garlic naan"—RC

603 Fort Washington Avenue, Washington Heights MN 10040
kismatindiannyc.com • +1 2127958633
Open 7 days • $$$$

MUSEUM EATS

New York is home to some of the richest museums in the world, many of which are a must-visit. Eating at a museum's restaurant or café can be so much more than grabbing a quick bite of sustenance between exhibitions, especially if you keep the following in mind:

– Museum eats are a lot more fun if you think of them as carefully prepared meals, rather than all-you-can-eat buffets; make a selection and then savour each bite. There's no crime in not tasting it all.

– Over the last decade, New York's museum restaurants have become destination restaurants – they're excellent.

– Excellent comes with a price tag, so museums with showcase restaurants also have more affordable café options.

For example, you might treat yourself to brunch at Untitled (page 82), the excellent restaurant on the ground floor of The Whitney, and then let the museum behave as a visual *digestivo*. Or, start on the 8th floor, with a light meal or cocktail at the more casual but also excellent Studio Café (page 83).

Alternatively, you could fight the crowds into the MoMA, enjoy an exhibition and then head to lunch at The Modern, its two-Michelin-star restaurant (page 80), or Café 2, which has a bustling vibe and long, communal tables. Either way, you'll feel fortified to continue on. (And when you finally emerge onto the street later, feeling peckish, cross Sixth Avenue to the red-and-yellow Halal Guys cart and enjoy a falafel or a gyro plate, perched on the fountain edge outside the Crédit Agricole bank. It's a New York tradition.)

Similar strategies may be applied at the Brooklyn Museum, which offers both The Norm (page 84), a restaurant in the oh-so-capable hands of Michelin-starred chef Saul Bolton, and a pleasant cafeteria that nods to the farmers' market up the street.

The Metropolitan Museum is something of an exception, as it's without an excellent restaurant. But it does have a summer rooftop bar (page 83) with sensational views, and options like the American Wing Café, where one can enjoy a sandwich or a slice of cake while marvelling at how they managed to install the limestone façade of the United States' Second Branch Bank inside the glass-enclosed garden of the Charles Engelhard Court.

The Met Breuer – the Met's modern art collection, now at home in the Whitney's old building – partly atones for this, with the Flora Bar (page 83), a posh space from chef Ignacio Mattos, with pricey small dishes, an extensive wine list and a sister called Flora Coffee, for those content to take their brutalist architecture with just takeaway sandwiches and pastry.

65 The Modern at the MoMA

Recommended by Michelle Maisto

"The Modern, from chef Danny Meyer, has two Michelin stars, three stars from *The New York Times* and a view of the museum's Sculpture Garden. Not persuaded to drop serious cash? Consider Bar Room at The Modern (it's much more lively than the restaurant), Terrace 5 (a full-service café, with a bird's-eye view of the garden) or the more communal-feeling Café 2 (an Italian restaurant and museum restorative masquerading as a cafeteria)"—*MM*

9 West 53rd Street, Midtown MN 10019
themodernnyc.com • +1 2123331220
Closed Sunday • $$$$

66 Untitled at the Whitney

Recommended by Michelle Maisto

"A few years ago, the Whitney moved downtown to a spot along the Hudson. Among the new Whitney's many gifts to the city is an excellent restaurant in a bustling, tourist-attracting neighbourhood known for – how to say this? – youthful carousing. Everything about Untitled, from the table settings to the house-made jam and the roasted and fried chicken, feels like the result of many thoughtful decisions. Every time I go I'm surprised and delighted"—*MM*

99 Gansevoort Street, West Village MN 10014
untitledatthewhitney.com • +1 2125703670
Open 7 days • $$$$

67 Flora Bar at the Met Breuer

Recommended by Vinh Nguyen, Roberto Serrini

"Ignacio's food can be truly inspirational... Seems fitting that it's attached to an art museum, ya know?"—*VN*

"A seafood-focused restaurant in a lofty, modern space at the Met Breuer. I love all of co-owner and chef Ignacio Mattos's restaurants. He's so dedicated and creative in his approach to cooking, as well as being an all-round nice guy"—*RS*

945 Madison Avenue, Upper East Side MN 10021
metmuseum.org • +1 6465585383
Closed Monday • $$$$

68 Cantor Roof Garden Bar at the Met

Recommended by Michelle Maisto

"Weather permitting, the Cantor Roof Garden Bar is open on Fridays from 5pm to 8pm from late May to early September. (There's also a Members Roof Garden Bar.) More than just a place to sip and take in the view, it's home to site-specific installations, making it a win-win-win destination"—*MM*

1000 5th Avenue, Upper East Side MN 10028
metmuseum.org • +1 2125703711
Hours variable • $$$$

69 Studio Café at the Whitney

Recommended by Roberto Serrini

"The patio at the new Whitney with a nice bottle of rosé and a fine day cannot be beat"—*RS*

99 Gansevoort Street, West Village MN 10014
untitledatthewhitney.com • +1 2125703670
Closed Tuesday • $$$$

70 The Norm at Brooklyn Museum

Recommended by Michelle Maisto

"Chef Saul Bolton has a long, celebrated history in Brooklyn. With The Norm, he takes inspiration from the diversity of the borough, offering dishes inspired by India, Mexico, the Caribbean, Japan, the Middle East and America's own cuisine. While there's a quick café in the breezeway beside it, The Norm also welcomes diners for small bites – a good excuse to sit and view priceless paintings, displayed in crates behind glass, as though the restaurant doubled as a culinary storage space"—MM

200 Eastern Parkway,
Prospect Heights BK 11238
thenormbkm.com • +1 7182300897
Open Thursday to Sunday • $$$$

SPECIAL OCCASION

Every New Yorker with a love of good food but not a bottomless bank account keeps a running mental (if not literal) list of restaurants for the occasion of, say, winning a major award that includes a meal at the restaurant of their choice. Or when they hit a milestone birthday. Or when very generous-feeling parents come to visit. (Yes, many adult New Yorkers still want their parents to take them to dinner – do you know what rents are in this town?)

For such special occasions – and a first-time visit to the city certainly qualifies – there are a handful of epicurean bastions you may want to plan for well in advance. These aren't restaurants one stumbles across but rather gleefully prepares for.

In possibly every instance, they're the vision of a chef – the embodiment of an ideology and ego, as much as any building is an architect's assertion. But they vary in cuisine and mood. While surprises are nice, an online search can offer worthwhile advice about signature dishes, cancellation policies and what to expect.

Can't justify the expense? Consider that these spiffy places nearly always have a companion restaurant, café or bar, offering – more or less literally – a taste of the larger experience, but with smaller demands on one's time and budget.

That all said, *special* shouldn't be defined by dollar signs. It's about finding a place that embodies the energy you're going for – whether that's high-end, down home or absolutely unique (hello, Sammy's Roumanian, page 90). So, raise a glass, and cheers to you!

⑦¹ INSA

Recommended by Vinh Nguyen

"If I were to throw a birthday party for myself, I'd go to INSA for some serious Korean barbecue and karaoke. Their slogan says it all... 'Korean Fun Time Place For Celebration'"—*VN*

328 Douglass Street, Gowanus BK 11217
insabrooklyn.com • +1 7188552620
Open 7 days • $$$$

72 Per Se

Recommended by Michelle Maisto

"Thomas Keller may be better known for his Napa Valley French-American restaurant, The French Laundry, but at Per Se – a New American restaurant – he offers a nine-course tasting menu in which no ingredient is repeated ($325). There's also a vegetarian version (same price). The menu changes constantly, but one always-present signature dish is 'Oysters and Pearls' – warm caviar and oysters under a savoury tapioca pudding"—MM

Time Warner Center, 10 Columbus Circle, Upper West Side MN 10023
thomaskeller.com • +1 2128239335
Open 7 days • $$$$

73 Blue Hill

Recommended by Michelle Maisto

"Blue Hill is a bucket-list restaurant for the type of person who loves beautiful, careful, high-end cuisine and also do-gooder agriculture (chef Dan Barber created the travelling pop-up, wastED, which featured dishes from ingredients like fish cartilages, normally destined for the trash). Blue Hill's Upstate sister restaurant, Blue Hill at Stone Barns, includes a working farm and educational centre, which largely inform the Blue Hill menu. It's all about seasonal, sustainable and artisanal"—MM

75 Washington Place, West Village MN 10011
bluehillfarm.com • +1 2125390959
Open 7 days • $$$$

74 Gallow Green

Recommended by Roberto Serrini

"Try Gallow Green at the McKitrick if the kids are not in town with you and wanna get a bit sexy"—*RS*

The five floors of the McKittrick Hotel are home to Sleep No More, the sans-spoken word, award-winning theatrical experience. But the roof of the McKittrick is host to Gallow Green, a verdant rooftop bar and restaurant with the vibe of a seductive, secret fairy garden. Head online to procure tickets for its weekend brunch.

542 West 27th Street, Chelsea MN 10001
mckittrickhotel.com • +1 2125641662
Open 7 days • $$$$

75 Famous Sammy's Roumanian Steakhouse

Recommended by Roberto Serrini

"Try Sammy's Roumanian if you are with a wild bunch who feel like eating in some random grandmother's wood panelled basement as Uncle Irving makes borderline racist comments while taking swigs from a bottle of vodka frozen in a block of ice"—*RS*

157 Chrystie Street, Lower East Side MN 10002
sammysromanian.com • +1 2126730330
Open 7 days • $$$$

76 Strip House

Recommended by Roberto Serrini

"My go-to for any special occasion because they do the world's best steak, with service that makes you feel like a king. Danny Meyer is a genius"—*RS*

15 West 44th Street, Midtown MN 10036
(see website for other locations)
striphouse.com • +1 2123365454
Open 7 days • $$$$

77 Sammy's Fish Box

Recommended by Raquel Cepeda

"I absolutely love Sammy's Fish Box on City Island and have been going there for family-centric occasions since I was a kid"—*RC*

41 City Island Avenue, City Island BX 10464
sammysfishbox.com • +1 7188850920
Open 7 days • $$$$

ICE CREAM

In every season, New Yorkers scream for ice cream, and those calls are answered with exacting ingredients, tremendous style and globally inspired creations.

So avoid the blue-and-white trucks with their noxious, toddler-height exhaust pipes – they peddle packaged, artificially coloured popsicles and cones of soft-serve made from ingredients like corn syrup, polysorbates and calcium sulphate (a close relation, literally, of wall plaster). Instead, open your phone's GPS and look around – excellent ice cream is everywhere.

There are dozens of shops that specialise in small-batch, organic and locally sourced ingredients. Examples include Van Leeuwen (page 98), Ample Hills, Blue Marble, Big Gay Ice Cream, Mikey Likes It, Davey's and Morgenstern's (page 94); many have multiple locations, as well as trucks you can search out on Twitter.

If you don't eat eggs, look for the moniker "Philadelphia Style". Made without a custard base, it's lighter, fluffier and – unimpeded by rich yolks – lets flavours shine through more. If gelato is your thing, head for a shop that does *only* that. (Gelato is more milk- than cream-based and is served at a lower temperature – it requires a separate freezer to ice cream.)

If you're less interested in assurances of hormone-free milk than in ice cream disrupted, head toward Manhattan's Chinatown (page 34), where frozen desserts are meeting with every kind of Asian influence. Think *ube* (purple yam) ice cream, Hong Kong-style egg waffle cones, shaved snow, *halo-halo* (shaved ice) and ice-cream-roll sundaes made on frozen cold plates while you watch. They're as much theatre and Instagram fodder as they are outstanding desserts.

78 Milk Bar

Recommended by Raquel Cepeda

"Milk Bar is where I go to have my absolute favourite ice cream: cereal milk with crunch"—*RC*

What Christina Tosi began essentially as a sweet complement to David Chang's Ssam Bar, has developed into an obsessively loved untraditional-dessert empire. Tosi's earliest creations – cereal milk soft-serve, crack pie and the compost cookie – are still some of her most beloved.

74 Christopher Street, West Village MN 10014
(see website for other locations)
milkbarstore.com • +1 3475779504
Open 7 days • $$$

SORBET ·v.

APRICOT
COCONUT
LYCHEE RASPBERRY

PINEAPPLE ORANGE
STRAWBERRY GUAVA

CUP/CONE		MONSTER CONE	
1 DIP	$4.50	1 DIP	$5.50
2 DIPS	$6.75	2 DIPS	$7.75
3 DIPS	$8.50	3 DIPS	$9.50
CUP+CONE AD 2 5			

DRINKS

HOUSE SODAS	$2.5
FLOATS	$8
SHAKES	$12
COOLERS	$8
AFFOGATOS	$6.5

79 Morgenstern's Finest Ice Cream

Recommended by Laura Ferrara

"I love the ice cream at Morgenstern's and go there for the creative flavours and top quality ingredients"—*LF*

2 Rivington Street, Lower East Side MN 10002
morgensternsnyc.com • +1 2122097684
Open 7 days • $$$$

TOPPINGS

RAMEL
ARAMEL

REAM
E SHOTS
E CHUNKS

INEAPPLE
CHERRIES
COCONUT

PICOSOS PEANUTS
ALEPPO PECANS
PISTACHIOS
TOASTED ALMONDS
WALNUTS
BLACK WALNUTS
SESAME HONEYCOMB
CASHEWS
HONEYED CASHEWS
JUNIOR MINTS
LEMON JAM
CONDENSED MILK

ALL TOPPINGS .50 EACH

KIDS'

CONE/CUP   4
MINI MORGENSTERN 7.5
BUTTERSCOTCH
    BANGER   6.5
LITTLE LION
    HEARTED   6.5

SERVED 8AM
TO 12 NOON

AVOCADO TOAST
$6.5

COFFEE
COUNTER CULTURE

COFFEE   2/2.
ESPRESSO   2.5
AMERICANO   2.5
CAFE AU LAIT   2.5
CAPPUCCINO   3.5
CORTADO   3.25
LATTE   4
MACCHIATO   3
MOCHA   5

HOT CHOCOLATE   3.5
TEA   2.5/3

ICED   + .5

80 Snowdays

Recommended by Michelle Maisto

"Snowdays (there are now six locations) represents the evolution of Taiwanese and Korean shaved ices. The cream comes from organic Hudson Valley dairies, and once shaved it's met with an avalanche of toppings. Options include American-style flavours and drizzles (NY Cheesecake, chocolate sauce, Nilla Wafers), but it's the Asian flavour combinations (roasted black sesame, red bean, grass jelly, condensed milk) that make it worth the trip"—*MM*

214 Flatbush Avenue,
Fort Green BK 11217
(see website for other locations)
snowdaysnyc.com • +1 3472940267
Open 7 days • $$$$

㊁ Van Leeuwen

Recommended by Olivia & Jennie, Roberto Serrini

"You'll never remember the name but you will remember their rum raisin for ever"—*RS*

172 Ludlow Street, Lower East Side MN 10014
(see website for other locations)
vanleeuwenicecream.com • +1 6468691746
Open 7 days • $$$

82   L&B Spumoni Gardens

Recommended by Laura Ferrara

"Spumoni Gardens in Brooklyn has been in business since 1939. Most people don't actually know what Spumoni is – it's a moulded Italian ice cream made with layers of different colours and flavours, usually containing candied fruits and nuts. They're also famous for their square Sicilian slice, which is worth a trip to the heart of Brooklyn"—*LF*

2725 86th Street, Gravesend BK 11223
spumonigardens.com • +1 7184491230
Open 7 days • $$$$

. . . .

83   Sundaes and Cones

Recommended by Alana Hoye Barnaba

"A milkshake from Sundaes and Cones hits the spot, especially on hotter days"—*AHB*

95 East 10th Street, East Village MN 10003
sundaescones.com • +1 2129799398
Open 7 days • $$$$

FOOD TRUCKS & PICNICS

New Yorkers love to picnic, particularly in parks and green spaces with skyscraper views. A theory: The city-country dichotomy makes a person feel, however fleetingly, like she has it all. Insert a few pork belly skewers, or a citrus-scented cup of ceviche, and who can argue with that?

Helping the cause is the fact that clever humans have figured out how to sell every imaginable treat out of food trucks and mobile stalls, from Russian dumplings to Brussels-style waffles and Neapolitan pizzas. (It may need to be said that these trucks have minimal in common with the food trucks of the 80s and 90s – or *roach coaches*, as they were better known. They're now essentially restaurants with "tiny house" lifestyles.)

If you have something in particular in mind, download an app like the *Roaming Hunger Food Truck Finder* – it shows what's around you in real time and later in the day. Twitter is also a good resource (search using hashtags), as many trucks tweet their locations.

Food truck fare is perfect for carrying into parks for impromptu picnicking, but many vendors are already there. On the weekends, thousands of people, and approximately 100 vendors, head to Smorgasburg (opposite) – on Saturdays in Williamsburg, on the East River State Park waterfront; on Sundays in Park Slope's Prospect Park, on Breeze Hill; and Fridays through Sundays at Smorg Square, in southern Manhattan, at the picnic-y corners of Varick and Canal.

Far from gathering in support of an event, the food *is* the event, and a competitive one for the vendors. People socialise and graze, moving from one stand to the next, looking for that next delicious bite.

See also Zabar's (page 124)

84 Saigon Vietnamese Sandwich Deli

Recommended by Alana Hoye Barnaba

I get a chicken *banh mi* from Saigon Vietnamese Sandwich Deli for lunch every week. It is the perfect lunch on the go"—*AHB*

369 Broome Street, Lower East Side MN 10013
banhmi.nyc • +1 2122198341
Open 7 days • $$$$

85 Sahadi 187

Recommended by Karl Wilder

"Great food counter with olive bar. Lebanon and other countries with similar food are represented here. I buy bags of prepared items to put together a quick meal when I'm eating late and not in the mood to cook"—*KW*

187 Atlantic Avenue, Brooklyn Heights BK 11201
sahadis.com • +1 7186244550
Open 7 days • $$$$

86 Smorgasburg

Recommended by Michelle Maisto

"Smorgasburg is a free, food-centric event. Bring cash, a refillable water bottle (disposable bottles aren't allowed), perhaps a picnic blanket and most definitely a big appetite, some patience and a sense of humour"—*MM*

76 Varick Street, Soho MN 10013
(see website for other locations)
smorgasburg.com
Open Friday to Sunday • $$$$

87 Union Fare

Recommended by Roberto Serrini

"I really like grabbing a poké bowl from the Gastrohall at Union Fare on 17th. UF is a great place because it's kind of a food court on hipster steroids; smashes, roast chickens, burgers, wood-fired pizzas – they basically have anything you want to eat and it's all fantastically good and quick"—*RS*

7 East 17th Street,
Gramercy MN 10003
unionfare.com • +1 2126336003
Open 7 days • $$$$

88 Lobster Place

Recommended by Alana Hoye Barnaba

"An all-time favourite spot for seafood is actually not a sit-down restaurant but Lobster Place in the huge indoor food hall, Chelsea Market. It is the best spot for a succulent steamed lobster"—*AHB*

Chelsea Market, 75 9th Avenue, Chelsea MN 10011
lobsterplace.com • +1 2122555672
Open 7 days • $$$$

COCKTAILS

Cocktails used to be considered somewhat feminine. The idea being that real drinkers drank "real drinks" (bourbon, neat!) and cocktails were for the folks who needed sugar and a little umbrella to get in on the party. Or else, they've meant drinks like Jack and Coke – with a lime, if the bartender was feeling fancy.

A culture shift began around 2000 that put a focus on cocktails that is every bit as serious and dedicated as the culinary endeavours applied to meats, cheeses and ice cream. It involves advanced preparations (reductions of juices and the creation of fun, simple syrups, say) and the hunting down of very specific spirits. A good barkeep should be able to speak with some knowledge about the bottles behind him or her. And a marvellous cocktail should be unexpectedly delicious, with tastes or textures that may surprise.

So look for a menu designed by a mixologist (there'll be a name somewhere on it). Or more exactly, a menu designed by someone clearly interested in creating delicious, interesting tastes and flavour combinations, using real ingredients you could recognise – fruits, vegetables, herbs, sugar cubes, eggs. (Cocktails are maybe the most fun sort of science.)

Where to go? Ignore self-important places with red ropes, places too dark or loud for you to have a conversation with the person taking your order, places that offer drinks in vessels compared to fishbowls, or places with rude staff. Cocktails are civilised, lovely and – plainly – fun! The same can be said of the best places that serve them.

89 Irvington

Recommended by Raquel Cepeda

"Irvington on the ground floor of The W Hotel is cool" —*RC*

This bar and restaurant on the ground floor of The W Hotel in Union Square (across from the city's most popular greenmarket, page 127) pays tribute to both the market and some classic Americana (Washington Irving, who penned *The Legend of Sleepy Hollow*, grew up in Manhattan). Expect a clean design, a seasonal menu, local ingredients and very capable bar service.

201 Park Avenue South, Gramercy MN 10003
irvingtonnyc.com • +1 2126770425
Open 7 days • $$$$

⑨⁰ Dead Rabbit Grocery and Grog

Recommended by Alana Hoye Barnaba

"Dead Rabbit Grocery and Grog offers a very unique vibe. There are interesting stories all around you and the drinks are excellent too!"—*AHB*

30 Water Street, Financial District MN 10004
deadrabbitnyc.com • +1 6464227906
Open 7 days • $$$$

91 Hotel Delmano

Recommended by Michelle Maisto, Vinh Nguyen

"A beautiful, Gatsby-esque bar with the first absinthe dripper many of us had ever seen. It's lovely and exciting and otherworldly, like being dropped in an old French film. Which, it's possible, may also be the doing of its excellent cocktails, both on the list and off the cuffs of its moustachioed bartenders" —MM

"It's my favourite place and I hope it's around forever. I bring all my friends and family here. The wines and cocktails are so good. I like going here with my wife, but if she's busy I know I'll have a nice time with the adorable staff"—VN

82 Berry Street, Williamsburg BK 11211
hoteldelmano.com • +1 7183871945
Open 7 days • $$$$

92 The Ides at Wythe Hotel

Recommended by Alex French, Vinh Nguyen

"I can't stand lines. But if you want to queue, the views at the Wythe Hotel are amazing"—VN

The Ides bar sits atop the Wythe hotel in the thick of hipster Williamsburg, offering – even from inside, on winter days – unobstructed views of the Manhattan skyline. The queue is likely to be long but they accept table reservations for up to seven guests (and those with table reservations don't pay the $10 entry fee). It's a gratuity-free establishment – no tipping, please.

80 Wythe Avenue, Williamsburg BK 11249
wythehotel.com • +1 7184608000
Open 7 days • $$$$

93 Maison Premiere

Recommended by Marisel Salazar

"Enjoy an artfully crafted cocktail in the lush garden outside on balmier days"—*MS*

Maison Premiere is a respite from the crush of Bedford Avenue. This plain-fronted, self-described "Oyster House and Cocktail Den" simultaneously evokes the French countryside and a bygone New York City, with a fern-draped backyard that is all New Orleans. The house drink is an Absinthe Colada – a very Williamsburg take on the Pina Colada.

298 Bedford Avenue, Williamsburg BK 11249
maisonpremiere.com • +1 3473350446
Open 7 days • $$$$

94 Two E Bar

Recommended by Alex French

"I enjoy happy hours in the Two E Bar at the Pierre, a hotel on Central Park East and 61st Street. The other patrons are meticulously turned out. The barman is capable. The chandeliered room is all plush carpet and small, candlelit tables arranged in a soothing, radiating symmetry. The bar, marvellously backlit, is flanked by vases of palm fronds or (in the spring) cherry blossoms"—*AF*

The Pierre Hotel, 2 East 61st Street, Midtown MN 10065
tajhotels.com • +1 2129408113
Open 7 days • $$$$

95 Salon de Ning

Recommended by Alex French

"Rooftop drinking is a genre all its own: more optimistic and less tethered to reality than ground-floor bacchanalia. Spritzes and aperitivos constructed of bitter Italian liquors and bubbles, cobblers, smashes and swizzles are best consumed at high altitude. Bad mojitos and oaky chardonnay should be avoided. When I'm feeling flush, Salon de Ning, atop the Peninsula Hotel, is my strong preference. Get a Negroni"—*AF*

23rd Floor, The Peninsula Hotel, 700 5th Avenue, Midtown MN 10019
newyork.peninsula.com • + 1 2129033097
Open 7 days • $$$$

96 Grand Bar

Recommended by Raquel Cepeda

"I like the Soho Grand Hotel because I can have a meeting over a cocktail in a relaxed setting"—*RC*

Soho Grand Hotel, 310 West Broadway, Soho MN 10013
sohogrand.com • +1 2129653588
Open 7 days • $$$$

HOT DRINKS

Coffee is personal. *Anything* one does in the hours before they have spoken aloud to another adult is personal. Which is to say, however you like your coffee, go for it. There's nothing you can't find in this city.

But if you have very exacting coffee standards, there is very exacting coffee to be found. One way is to look for a shop with "Coffee Roasters" in its name. More than a dozen independent coffee brands roast their coffees in the city – and sell at their cafés and others' – which certainly bodes well for a good cup.

If you're in a shop that takes its beans seriously, a great, simple option is a pour-over. It takes a few extra minutes, but you'll be getting a pure expression of the beans. An Aeropress coffee is another great option. Or, if they have one (and if so, lucky you and well done!) a Japanese Siphon.

How to know if a shop takes its beans seriously? If it sells roasted coffees by the bag (likely roasted by the partners on their menu, if not by themselves) take a look. Is it Arabica? (Robusta is a lower quality plant, mostly used for the pre-ground coffees in tin cans at the grocery store.) And is there a roasting date stamped on the bag? Ideally, it should be within two weeks of the current date. No date? Red flag.

Lastly, take a look in the shop's glass case to check out its pastry game. Because the best way to take your coffee is with some delicious company.

If tea is your thing, you likely already know what you're after. Plenty of shops can offer a tea bag, and some of these are better than others. But a shop that takes tea seriously will offer it by the pot.

See also Kopitiam (page 39)

97 Café Colette

Recommended by Vinh Nguyen

"I think Café Colette is a cool place to get some coffee and people-watch. My hands shake enough without a cup of joe, so I just tag along and look at the coffee junkies"—*VN*

79 Berry Street, Williamsburg BK 11249
cafe-colette.com • +1 3475991381
Open 7 days • $$$$

98 CHOCnyc

Recommended by Raquel Cepeda

"I like CHOCnyc in my neighbourhood (and always with a pastry because, why not?)" —*RC*

A high-end bakery, CHOCnyc was created by Brad Doles, a hospitality veteran, and Jemal Edwards, a pastry chef who has worked in France, Austria, Italy and Japan. They offer everything from croissants and scones to cookies, macarons and elegant birthday cakes.

4996 Broadway, Inwood MN 10034
chocnyc.com
Open 7 days • $$$

99 Abraço

Recommended by Roberto Serrini

"Hands down best latte in the world. Tastes like cake"—*RS*

Abraço is a family effort. It's an espresso bar, a coffee roaster, a purveyor of house-made pastries and savouries, and a beloved neighbourhood jewel. And though it recently moved to larger digs across the street, it still has the feel of being a little place, bursting with big, happy energy.

81 East 7th Street, East Village MN 10003
abraconyc.com
Closed Monday • $$$$

100 Konditori

Recommended by Alex French

"Konditori – a Swedish chain of coffee shops with eight locations from Brooklyn to Manhattan – serves strong, flavourful, painstakingly prepared coffee drinks in a setting of Scandinavian simplicity. It's caffeine done right" —*AF*

182 Allen Street, Lower East Side MN 10002
(see website for other locations)
konditori.com
Open 7 days • $$$$

101 City of Saints

Recommended by Michelle Maisto

"City of Saints has coffee shops in Hoboken, Manhattan's East Village and Brooklyn's Bushwick neighbourhood, where it roasts all the meticulously sourced beans for its shops and wholesale customers. The cafés are pleasantly hip and the coffee – single-origins and two outstanding house blends – is excellent. A bag of roasted beans is a worthwhile souvenir"—*MM*

79 East 10th Street, East Village MN 10003
(see website for other locations)
cityofsaintscoffee.com • +1 6465901624
Open 7 days • $$$$

102 Té Company

Recommended by Laura Ferrara

"I love this place. Elena Liao and her husband, Frederico Ribeiro, make the most delicious food in the tiniest place. It's not commercialised, it's just a small place offering only oolong tea and small bites. Elena and Frederico create the most beautiful music together, with her knowledge of the most fascinating teas and his Portuguese flavours – it's a beautiful marriage of cultures. Ribeiro is an alum of Per Se and Il Buco, and he occasionally serves a pop-up tasting menu and tea-pairing dinner called Dinner at Bonnie's, a tribute to Bonnie Slotnick Cookbooks, which previously occupied this West Village space"—*LF*

163 West 10th Street, West Village MN 10014
te-nyc.com • +1 9293353168
Closed Monday • $$$$

GROCERIES & GIFTS

When it comes to groceries, New Yorkers are like magpies, patching together menus from farmers' market stalls, Amazon orders, the corner bodega and the rare, large grocery store.

But when in need of something special, whether for a dinner party menu, a gift or a treat, a second roster of shops are called upon. Some are cutely curated mish-mashes, others highly focused – such as cheese stores, or fish stores – and still others are sprawling adventures that are day trips in themselves. They *may* have startling price tags in common. What they *must* have is an atmosphere and a shopping experience that surprises and delights, making it (almost) finally true that it's as fun to give as to receive.

What makes a good gift depends on the recipient – and the length of your journey home. But if you're after something *Made In New York*, options include beer, wine, taffy candy, chocolates, crackers, granolas, pickles, jams and a number of spirits from a handful of craft distilleries. (Many of these are in Brooklyn, and many– including the New York Distilling Co., Kings County Distillery, Van Brunt Stillhouse and Industry City – offer tasting tours.)

New Yorkers have an old reputation for being rude, but that's largely a myth. Don't ever hesitate to ask for help or advice, particularly in a speciality shop. Someone – or more likely, many, many people – put their heart and hours of attention into making selections. Chances are excellent they'll be thrilled to get into details with you, point you to something you might not have seen or offer you a taste.

See also Fei Long Market Food Court (page 39), New World Mall (page 35)

103 Roni-Sue's Chocolates

Recommended by Alana Hoye Barnaba

"The chocolate covered bacon (aka pig candy) from Roni-Sue's Chocolates makes great gifts"—AHB

148 Forsyth Street, Lower East Side MN 10002
roni-sue.com • +1 2126771216
Closed Wednesday • $$$$

104 Eataly

Recommended by Michelle Maisto

"Mario Batali's Eataly, at nearly the size of a football field, is the food-lover's equivalent of Willy Wonka's factory. Every direction holds an enticing diversion – a cheese shop! a pizza counter! a wine bar! a gelato stand! There are sit-down restaurants and casual-ish stand-up tables where waiters deliver drinks and aperitivo. And of course, if there's an Italian grocery item you'd like to shop for, expect an aisle or a display of the finest options"—*MM*

200 5th Avenue, Flatiron MN 10010
(see website for other locations)
eataly.com • +1 2122292560
Open 7 days • $$$$

105 D. Coluccio and Sons

Recommended by Laura Ferrara

"For Italian speciality food – the owners are third generation"—*LF*

1214 60th Street, Borough Park BK 11219
dcoluccioandsons.com • +1 7184366700
Open 7 days • $$$$

arma Prosciutto Boneless	Italian Provolone Fiaschetto	Italian Provolone Extra Piccante	Sicilian Canestrato & Pepato Aged	D.O.P Ragusano Caciocavallo Aged	Riserva Grana Padano	Parmigiano Reggiano Aged Over 24 Months	Italian Genuine Pecorino Romano
.95 lb 12.95 lb	7.25 lb	8.95 lb	10.95 lb	11.95 lb	9.95 lb	12.95 lb	7.75 lb

106 PJ Wine

Recommended by Raquel Cepeda

"I buy drink-related gifts at PJ Wine in my neighbourhood. Their selection is like no other in the city. It's not fussy, so I can peruse and chill, there's always someone knowledgeable to consult with, and their prices are the lowest I've seen anywhere in New York"—*RC*

4898 Broadway, Inwood MN 10034
pjwine.com • +1 2125675500
Open 7 days • $$$$

---

107 Zabar's

Recommended by Karl Wilder

"One of the few good bagels left in NY and a killer prepared-foods deli. I can find real olive oil, rare cheeses, handmade pastas and every type of kitchen supply. It is a foodie dream store. You can get an entire picnic and go to Central Park and pig out. Locally they are called the Temple of Cheese due to their extensive international cheese collection"—*KW*

2245 Broadway, Upper West Side MN 10024
zabars.com • +1 2127872000
Open 7 days • $$$$

---

108 Sahadi's

Recommended by Michelle Maisto

"More wallet-friendly than Eataly (page 120), but just as transportive, are the aisles of Sahadi's, a Middle Eastern grocery store in Cobble Hill that's filled with packaged goods and jars, bins, tins, tubs, barrels and baskets of everything from roasted coffee beans to olives, spices, chocolates, dried fruit, cheeses and caramels. Everything is an excuse to go back"—*MM*

187 Atlantic Avenue, Brooklyn Heights BK 11201
sahadis.com • +1 7186244550
Open 7 days • $$$$

109 Fairway

Recommended by Raquel Cepeda

"I find myself frequenting Fairway because it's convenient and varied"—*RC*

Fairway is arguably New York City's most beloved "grocery store", a phrase that hardly captures the stunning wealth and quality of all it offers. Each store is different, but its first location – opened in the 1930s, on the Upper West Side – is classic New York. The cheese section alone is worth a visit, there's a café for coffee and a light lunch, and an upstairs for perusing housewares.

2131 Broadway, Upper East Side MN 10023
(see website for other locations)
fairwaymarket.com • +1 2125951888
Open 7 days • $$$$

GREENMARKETS

New York City has more than 60 farmers' markets (or *greenmarkets*, in the official parlance), where farmers, fishmongers, gardeners, millers, butchers, picklers, vintners, sheep shearers, pastry bakers, cheese makers and other artisans arrive early to sell their wares.

Some markets occur once a week and are small, utilitarian affairs, providing a portion of a neighbourhood with access to a handful of vendors offering local produce and perhaps fresh bread, just-caught fish, or pork or beef from local farms. Then there are the larger markets, which run two or three days each week – or four in the case of Union Square (opposite).

While likely the majority of New Yorkers have walked through the Union Square Greenmarket (it's a major subway hub, a connection point for multiple neighbourhoods and close to New York University life), it's common for New Yorkers to otherwise only know the one or two markets closest to their homes or maybe their offices. But these tiny markets can offer up gems, from peaches a few hours off the tree, to small-batch jars of apple butter.

The larger Saturday markets, such as Brooklyn's Grand Army Plaza (page 128) and Fort Greene Park (page 129), answer a need for groceries as much as for socialisation. People bring their dogs and baby strollers and reusable bags – and maybe compost to drop off at one tent and old textiles at another. They graze on free samples in the produce stalls and occasional cooking displays, sip their coffees to the backdrop of busking musicians, bump into neighbours, buy flowers for the dining table, a fresh fish, a bottle of Long Island wine, local cheese, fruit and vegetables, and perhaps some pickles, sausages, honey, Upstate yoghurt or a just-baked focaccia for lunch.

For a complete list of the markets and their dates and times, visit grownyc.org/greenmarket/ourmarkets.

🔟⁰ Union Square

Recommended by Raquel Cepeda, Laura Ferrara, Vinh Nguyen

"It's always bustling with people, and the smell of flowers and lavender wafting about makes me feel like I'm walking through a garden in the middle of the city"—*RC*

"It's the best! Real farmers, real local food. It's where some of the best chefs shop too so you know you're in good company. Plus they have all these artisans with their cheese, honey and baked goods... keepin' it REAL!"—*VN*

East 17th Street & Union Square West, Gramercy MN 10003
grownyc.org
Closed Tuesday, Thursday and Sunday • $$$$

⑪ Grand Army Plaza

Recommended by Michelle Maisto

"The Grand Army Plaza market sets up each Saturday at the head of Prospect Park, across the street from Brooklyn's Central Library and a short walk from the Botanic Garden and the Brooklyn Museum – all of which are common follow-ups after a visit to the market (for those who shop lightly). For many in Park Slope, the market is part of a committed routine – spring herb gardens sprout when the herb seedlings arrive on the market tables, and hearty autumn flowers fill window boxes when the market overflows with them. People go for fresh produce – fish, bread, cheese and meat – as well as to drop off food scraps for compost or old clothes for recycling. In good weather, it's mayhem, with dogs and bicycles and politicians and performers. And in winter, an abbreviated version continues, at a faster clip"—*MM*

Grand Army Plaza, Park Slope BK 11238
grownyc.org
Open Saturday • $$$$

⑫ Tucker Square

Recommended by Michelle Maisto

"The Tucker Square (aka Lincoln Center) greenmarket runs year-round each Thursday, across Broadway from the Metropolitan Opera and Ballet, in Tucker Square, which is basically a glorified central reservation. It's a small market with little folding tables set up under some trees, which eventually make for some lovely, dappled shade. A handful of dedicated, year-round farmers attend and another handful arrives during the growing season – with honey, raw cow's milk, fresh bread and flowers. Grab a fresh pastry, some local honey as a souvenir, and watch for the ballerinas hurrying to practice"—*MM*

West 66th Street & Broadway, Upper West Side MN 10023
grownyc.org
Open Saturday • $$$$

113 Fort Greene Park

Recommended by Michelle Maisto

"Attendance at Brooklyn's Fort Greene likely rivals Grand Army Plaza (opposite), but the longer, narrower, park-hugging shape of the market – and the trees providing direct shade – give it a very different feeling. It's green and lovely and an absolutely thorough market (anything offered at another market is sure to be offered here). It's also the only greenmarket where I've ever seen cherry pie muffins (I'm still dreaming of them) and live bees at the honey stand (ditto)"—MM

Dekalb Avenue Brooklyn, Fort Greene BK 11201
grownyc.org
Open Saturday • $$$$

RECIPES

Blueberry Pancakes

Smoked Salmon Bagel

Waldorf Salad

Reuben

Tuna Melt

Sesame Noodles

New York Cheesecake

Peanut Butter Shake

Manhattan

Cosmopolitan

Old Fashioned

Blueberry Pancakes

The perfect treat for a lazy-day breakfast.

Serves 2–3

200g plain flour

1 tbsp baking powder

1 tsp caster sugar

Pinch of salt

1 egg

300ml milk

100g blueberries, frozen or fresh, plus extra to serve

Butter, for frying, plus extra to serve

Maple or golden syrup, to serve

Mix the flour, baking powder, sugar and salt together in a bowl before whisking in the egg and milk. Don't worry if there are a few lumps, they'll dissipate as the mixture rests. Leave for at least 10 minutes (or up to 1 hour) to allow the gluten in the batter to relax (making for fluffier pancakes).

When you're ready to cook, put a wide frying pan over a medium heat and gently stir the blueberries into the batter.

When the pan is hot, add a small knob of butter and swirl to coat the base. Spoon a tablespoon or two of the batter into the pan and allow to spread to make one pancake. (If the pan is big enough you can make several at a time.) Cook for 2–3 minutes on each side until golden and bubbling.

Serve on warmed plates with extra butter, blueberries and lashings of maple or golden syrup.

Smoked Salmon Bagel

Toppings may vary from deli to deli, but the key components remain the same. If you like, you can pep up your cream cheese "schmear" by mixing in thinly sliced spring onions, some more salmon, or even caviar.

Serves 2

2 bagels

4 tbsp cream cheese

Enough smoked salmon to fill each bagel with two layers

Capers, finely chopped (optional)

Red onion, finely chopped (optional)

Dill, finely chopped (optional)

Halve and lightly toast the bagels then spread 1 tablespoon of cream cheese over all four halves.

Add the salmon to two of the bagel halves, followed by your choice of capers, onion or dill. Top each bagel with the other half and enjoy.

Waldorf Salad

Famously created at New York's Waldorf Astoria Hotel over 100 years ago, this simple salad bursting with flavour and texture makes for a super starter or light lunch.

Serves 2

3 tbsp mayonnaise

Juice of ½ lemon

1 apple, thinly sliced

Handful of grapes, halved

2 celery sticks, thinly sliced

Handful of walnut halves, toasted

A few lettuce leaves

Sea salt and freshly ground black pepper

Mix the mayonnaise and lemon juice together in a large bowl and season to taste with salt and pepper.

Add the apple, grapes and celery and toss gently until they are evenly coated with the dressing.

Crumble in the toasted walnuts and give the salad a final stir before arranging on the lettuce leaves. Serve immediately.

Reuben

With its salty beef and pickle-spiked dressing, this is the sandwich that dreams are made of.

Serves 2

4 thick slices of best quality bread (ideally rye or sourdough)

Butter, for spreading

6 thick slices of salt beef or pastrami

4 tbsp sauerkraut

4 slices of Swiss cheese (such as Gruyère or Emmental)

Gherkins, to serve

For the Russian dressing

2 tbsp mayonnaise

1 tbsp ketchup

2 tsp mustard or grated horseradish

½ small shallot, finely chopped

1 small gherkin, finely chopped

A dash of Worcestershire sauce

Sea salt and freshly ground black pepper

To make the Russian dressing, mix all the ingredients together in a small bowl and season to taste.

Set a wide frying pan over a medium-high heat.

To assemble, start by buttering both sides of all four slices of bread. Pile the Russian dressing onto two slices before layering on the beef or pastrami, then the sauerkraut and cheese slices.

Top with the remaining slices of bread and carefully transfer the sandwiches to your preheated frying pan. Heat for 3–4 minutes on each side until the bread is golden and crisp and the cheese has started to melt. Serve immediately with a few tangy gherkins.

Tuna Melt

Cheese on toast with the added bonus of tuna salad, this easy assembly job makes for a perfect midnight snack.

Serves 2

200g tin tuna, drained

A few spring onions, finely chopped

Juice of ½ lemon

4 tbsp mayonnaise

4 thick slices of granary, rye or sourdough bread

50g Cheddar or Gouda, grated

Sea salt and freshly ground black pepper

A few gherkins, to serve

Preheat the grill to high.

In a small bowl, mix together the tuna, spring onions, lemon juice and mayonnaise. Season to taste.

Divide the mixture evenly and spread onto the four slices of bread. Top with the grated cheese, place on a baking tray and grill until the cheese is melted and bubbling. Serve immediately with the gherkins alongside.

Sesame Noodles

A classic takeout dish from the city that never sleeps. Make extra, as the noodles taste equally good straight from the fridge.

Serves 4

250g dried medium egg noodles

Thumb-sized piece of ginger, finely grated

2 garlic cloves, finely grated

1 red chilli, finely chopped

2 tbsp sesame oil

4 tbsp soy sauce

2 tbsp tahini

1 tbsp peanut butter

1 tbsp sugar

½ cucumber, sliced into thin batons

30g peanuts, toasted and roughly chopped

Cook the noodles according to the packet instructions, then rinse with cold water and set aside.

In a large bowl, whisk together the ginger, garlic, chilli, sesame oil, soy sauce, tahini, peanut butter and sugar. Add the noodles and toss to coat. Transfer to a serving dish and garnish with the cucumber and peanuts.

New York Cheesecake

An authentic baked cheesecake that's creamy and satisfying. Serve plain or with a dollop of berry compote.

Serves 10

For the crust

75g butter, melted

150g digestive biscuits, blitzed to a fine crumb

For the filling

900g full-fat cream cheese

250g caster sugar

200ml sour cream

3 tbsp plain flour

3 large eggs, plus 1 egg yolk

1 tsp vanilla extract

Juice and zest of ½ lemon

Preheat the oven 180°C. Grease and line the base of a 23cm springform cake tin.

In a large bowl, mix the melted butter and biscuits until combined. Tip into the lined cake tin and press down evenly to form the base. Bake for 10 minutes then leave to cool while you prepare the filling.

Reduce the oven temperature to 160°C.

Beat together the cream cheese and sugar in a large bowl. Once smooth, beat in the sour cream and flour before gradually adding the eggs and egg yolk, one at a time. Add the vanilla extract to the bowl, along with the lemon zest and juice, and give the mixture a final stir.

Pour the mixture onto the cooled base and smooth the top. Bake for 50 minutes, until the cheesecake has set but retains a slight wobble. Turn off the oven, prop the door open and leave the cheesecake to cool completely before you remove it (this will help prevent the cheesecake's top from cracking).

Peanut Butter Shake

Retro, nostalgic flavours can be found everywhere in New York, especially when it comes to ice cream and milkshakes. This sumptuous and simple number ticks all the boxes and is the ideal treat for beating those post-holiday blues. The below is just a starting point. Feel free to get creative with different flavours of ice cream, chocolate sauce, whipped cream, nuts and fresh fruit.

Serves 1

2 scoops of vanilla ice cream

2 tablespoons peanut butter

A little milk, to loosen

Blitz the ingredients together in a blender until smooth and frothy. Pour into a tall glass and enjoy.

Manhattan

Though this heady cocktail's specific origins are contentious, there's no doubt that it's one of the finest exports of the city.

Serves 1

50ml whisky or bourbon

25ml sweet vermouth

2–3 dashes of Angostura bitters

1 Maraschino cherry, to decorate

Pour the whisky, vermouth and bitters into a tumbler, add plenty of ice and stir. Strain into a chilled martini glass and decorate with a cherry.

Cosmopolitan

Ubiquitous in the late nineties thanks to a certain television show, this fruity little number is still one of the best ways to get a party started.

Serves 1

40ml vodka

15ml orange liqueur, such as Cointreau

30ml cranberry juice

Squeeze of lime juice

Twist of orange, to decorate

Shake the vodka, orange liqueur, cranberry juice and lime juice together over ice then strain into a chilled martini glass. Decorate with a twist of orange.

Old Fashioned

Sometimes the old ones really are the best. This knock-your-socks-off drink is incredibly simple and, when mixed right, utter gold. Purists will often leave out the fruit but many consider it a fun addition to a typically serious drink.

Serves 1

1 sugar cube

2–3 dashes of Angostura bitters

50ml bourbon

Twist of orange, to decorate (optional)

1 Maraschino cherry, to decorate (optional)

Put the sugar cube into a tumbler and douse with the bitters and a few drops of water. Add the bourbon and stir until the sugar is dissolved. Fill the tumbler with large ice cubes and stir for about 20 seconds to chill. Decorate with the orange and cherry, if you like.

INDEX **A TO Z**

A

15 A&S Fine Foods
99 Abraço
58 ATLA

B

34 Babbalucci
8 Bagel Hole
42 Bar Primi
10 Black Seed Bagels
73 Blue Hill
51 Brindle Room
9 Brooklyn Bagel & Coffee
37 Brooklyn Firefly
53 Burger and Lobster
46 Burger Joint

C

97 Café Colette
2 Café Mogador
68 Cantor Roof Garden Bar at
   the Met
98 CHOCnyc
101 City of Saints
1 Clinton St. Baking Company

D

105 D. Coluccio and Sons
3 De Maria
90 Dead Rabbit Grocery and Grog
13 DeFonte's
20 Dominique Ansel Bakery
21 Doughnut Plant

E

104 Eataly
54 El Economico

F

109 Fairway
75 Famous Sammy's Roumanian
28 Fei Long Market Food Court
67 Flora Bar at the Met Breuer
113 Fort Greene Park
22 Fried Dumpling

G

74 Gallow Green
40 Giuseppina's
111 Grand Army Plaza
96 Grand Bar

H

59 Hanoi House
11 Harry and Ida's
30 Hasaki
45 Hearth
91 Hotel Delmano

I

44 I Sodi
92 The Ides at Wythe Hotel
61 Indochine
71 INSA
89 Irvington

J

49 J.G. Melon

K

33 Karasu
64 Kismat
100 Konditori
27 Kopitiam
31 Kyo Ya

L

82 L&B Spumoni Gardens
82 Lobster Place
38 Lucali's

M

93 Maison Premiere
5 El Malecon
29 Mama Sushi
78 Milk Bar
12 Minetta Tavern
65 The Modern at the MoMA
19 Molly's Cupcakes
79 Morgenstern's Finest Ice
   Cream

N

24 New World Mall
25 Nom Wah Tea Parlor
70 The Norm at Brooklyn
   Museum
55 La Nueva España

O

12 Oasis
32 Omen Azen

P

57 Panca
63 Patel Brothers
72 Per Se

16 Peter Pan Donuts
106 PJ Wine
62 Pongal
60 Pye Boat

R

36 Ribalta
103 Roni-Sue's Chocolates
7 Russ & Daughters

S

85 Sahadi 187
108 Sahadi's
84 Saigon Vietnamese
   Sandwich Deli
76 Salon de Ning
77 Sammy's Fish Box
35 Saraghina
6 Selamat Pagi
48 Shake Shack
86 Smorgasburg
80 Snowdays
47 The Spotted Pig
50 Springbone
52 Strip House
39 Stromboli Pizza
69 Studio Café at the Whitney
83 Sundaes and Cones

T

56 Los Tacos No. 1
102 Té Company
23 Thai Son
4 Tim Ho Wan
112 Tucker Square
94 Two E Bar

U

87 Union Fare
110 Union Square
66 Untitled at the Whitney

V

14 V-Nam Café
81 Van Leeuwen
17 Veniero's
43 Via Carota
18 Villabate Alba

X

26 Xi'an Famous Foods

Z

107 Zabar's
41 Zero Otto Nove

INDEX **BY LOCAL**

RAQUEL CEPEDA

37 Brooklyn Firefly
2 Café Mogador
98 CHOCnyc
109 Fairway
96 Grand Bar
89 Irvington
64 Kismat
29 Mama Sushi
Milk Bar
19 Molly's Cupcakes
55 La Nueva España
57 Panca
106 PJ Wine
77 Sammy's Fish Box
23 Thai Son
110 Union Square
14 V-Nam Café
41 Zero Otto Nove

LAURA FERRARA

15 A&S Fine Foods
10 Black Seed Bagels
105 D. Coluccio and Sons
3 De Maria
22 Fried Dumpling
30 Hasaki
44 I Sodi
61 Indochine
82 L&B Spumoni Gardens
79 Morgenstern's Finest Ice
   Cream
32 Omen Azen
35 Saraghina
47 The Spotted Pig
102 Té Company
110 Union Square
43 Via Carota
18 Villabate Alba

ALEX FRENCH

92 The Ides at Wythe Hotel
100 Konditori
12 Oasis
95 Salon de Ning
94 Two E Bar

ALANA HOYE BARNABA

53 Burger and Lobster
1 Clinton St. Baking Company
90 Dead Rabbit Grocery and Grog
20 Dominique Ansel Bakery
88 Lobster Place
25 Nom Wah Tea Parlor

103 Roni-Sue's Chocolates
84 Saigon Vietnamese
   Sandwich Deli
83 Sundaes and Cones

MICHELLE MAISTO

8 Bagel Hole
73 Blue Hill
46 Burger Joint
68 Cantor Roof Garden Bar at
   the Met
101 City of Saints
13 DeFonte's
21 Doughnut Plant
104 Eataly
28 Fei Long Market Food Court
113 Fort Greene Park
40 Giuseppina's
111 Grand Army Plaza
91 Hotel Delmano
65 The Modern at the MoMA
70 The Norm at Brooklyn
   Museum
63 Patel Brothers
72 Per Se
62 Pongal
108 Sahadi's
48 Shake Shack
86 Smorgasburg
80 Snowdays
4 Tim Ho Wan
112 Tucker Square
66 Untitled at the Whitney

VINH NGUYEN

58 ATLA
10 Black Seed Bagels
97 Café Colette
67 Flora Bar at the Met Breuer
59 Hanoi House
91 Hotel Delmano
92 The Ides at Wythe Hotel
71 INSA
49 J.G. Melon
33 Karasu
31 Kyo Ya
16 Peter Pan Donuts
7 Russ & Daughters
56 Los Tacos No. 1
110 Union Square

OLIVIA & JENNIE

10 Black Seed Bagels
81 Van Leeuwen
42 Bar Primi

MARISEL SALAZAR

27 Kopitiam
93 Maison Premiere
52 Minetta Tavern
6 Selamat Pagi
26 Xi'an Famous Foods

ROBERTO SERRINI

99 Abraço
51 Brindle Room
9 Brooklyn Bagel & Coffee
75 Famous Sammy's Roumanian
67 Flora Bar at the Met Breuer
74 Gallow Green
11 Harry and Ida's
Hearth
38 Lucali's
24 New World Mall
25 Nom Wah Tea Parlor
60 Pye Boat
36 Ribalta
76 Strip House
39 Stromboli Pizza
69 Studio Café at the Whitney
87 Union Fare
81 Van Leeuwen
17 Veniero's

KARL WILDER

34 Babbalucci
54 El Economico
5 El Malecon
85 Sahadi 187
50 Springbone
107 Zabar's

INDEX **BY NEIGHBOURHOOD**

BRONX

CITY ISLAND
77 Sammy's Fish Box

KINGSBRIDGE
54 El Economico

BROOKLYN

BAY RIDGE
37 Brooklyn Firefly

BEDFORD-STUYVESANT
35 Saraghina

BELMONT
41 Zero Otto Nove

BENSONHURST
18 Villabate Alba

BOROUGH PARK
105 D. Coluccio and Sons

BROOKLYN HEIGHTS
85 Sahadi 187
108 Sahadi's

FORT GREENE
113 Fort Greene Park
33 Karasu

GOWANUS
71 INSA

GRAVESEND
15 A&S Fine Foods
82 L&B Spumoni Gardens

GREENPOINT
16 Peter Pan Donuts
6 Selamat Pagi

GREENWOOD
40 Giuseppina's

PARK SLOPE
8 Bagel Hole
111 Grand Army Plaza

PROSPECT HEIGHTS
70 The Norm at Brooklyn Museum

RED HOOK
13 DeFonte's
38 Lucali's

SUNSET PARK
28 Fei Long Market Food Court

WILLIAMSBURG
97 Café Colette
91 Hotel Delmano
92 The Ides at Wythe Hotel
12 Maison Premiere
6 Oasis

MANHATTAN

CHELSEA
74 Gallow Green
88 Lobster Place
56 Los Tacos No. 1

CHINATOWN
22 Fried Dumpling
27 Kopitiam
11 Nom Wah Tea Parlor
23 Thai Son
26 Xi'an Famous Foods

EAST VILLAGE
99 Abraço
51 Brindle Room
2 Café Mogador
101 City of Saints
1 Clinton St. Baking Company
59 Hanoi House
11 Harry and Ida's
30 Hasaki
45 Hearth
61 Indochine
31 Kyo Ya
80 Snowdays
83 Sundaes and Cones
4 Tim Ho Wan
17 Veniero's

FINANCIAL DISTRICT
90 Dead Rabbit Grocery and Grog

FLATIRON
53 Burger and Lobster
104 Eataly
49 J.G. Melon
48 Shake Shack

GRAMERCY
42 Bar Primi
89 Irvington
36 Ribalta
39 Stromboli Pizza
87 Union Fare
110 Union Square

HARLEM
34 Babbalucci
29 Mama Sushi

INWOOD
98 CHOCnyc
55 La Nueva España
106 PJ Wine

LOWER EAST SIDE
21 Doughnut Plant
75 Famous Sammy's Roumanian
100 Konditori
79 Morgenstern's Finest Ice Cream
103 Roni-Sue's Chocolates

7 Russ & Daughters
84 Saigon Vietnamese
    Sandwich Deli
14 V-Nam Café

MIDTOWN
46 Burger Joint
65 The Modern at the MoMA
62 Pongal
95 Salon de Ning
76 Strip House
94 Two E Bar

NOLITA
58 ATLA
3 De Maria

SOHO
10 Black Seed Bagels
20 Dominique Ansel Bakery
9 Grand Bar
52 Minetta Tavern
32 Omen Azen
86 Smorgasburg
50 Springbone

UPPER EAST SIDE
68 Cantor Roof Garden Bar
109 Fairway
67 Flora Bar at the Met Breuer

UPPER WEST SIDE
5 El Malecon
78 Milk Bar
72 Per Se
112 Tucker Square
107 Zabar's

WASHINGTON HEIGHTS
64 Kismat

WEST VILLAGE
73 Blue Hill
44 I Sodi
19 Molly's Cupcakes
57 Panca
69 Studio Café at the Whitney
102 Té Company
66 Untitled at the Whitney
81 Van Leeuwen
43 Via Carota
47 The Spotted Pig

QUEENS

ASTORIA
9 Brooklyn Bagel & Coffee
60 Pye Boat

FLUSHING
24 New World Mall

JACKSON HEIGHTS
63 Patel Brothers

BLOOMSBURY PUBLISHING
Bloomsbury Publishing Plc
50 Bedford Square, London WC1B 3DP

BLOOMSBURY, BLOOMSBURY PUBLISHING and the Diana logo
are trademarks of Bloomsbury Publishing Plc

First published in Great Britain 2018

A catalogue record for this book is available from the British Library

ISBN: 978-1-4088-9327-2

2 4 6 8 10 9 7 5 3 1

Series Editor: Lena Hall
Contributing Writer: Michelle Maisto
Cover Designer: Greg Heinimann
Designer: Julyan Bayes
Photographer: Cayla Zahoran
Production Controller: Arlene Alexander

Printed and bound in China by RR Donnelley Asia Printing Solutions Ltd.

To find out more about our authors and books visit
www.bloomsbury.com and sign up for our newsletters

BRUNCH

1. Clinton St. Baking Co. — D3
2. Café Mogador — D4
3. De Maria — D2
4. Tim Ho Wan — E2
5. Malecon — I4
6. Selamat Pagi — E5

BAGELS

7. Russ & Daughters — E3
8. Bagel Hole — A3
9. Brooklyn Bagel & Coffee — G6
10. Black Seed Bagels — E3

SANDWICHES

11. Harry and Ida's — E3
12. Oasis — D4
13. DeFonte's — B2
14. V-Nam Café — E3
15. A&S Fine Foods — A3

DOUGHNUTS & PASTRIES

16. Peter Pan Donuts — E5
17. Veniero's — E3
18. Villabate Alba — A2
19. Molly's Cupcakes — E2
20. Dominique Ansel Bakery — E2
21. Doughnut Plant — D3

CHINATOWN

22. Fried Dumpling — D2
23. Thai Son — D2
24. New World Mall — G8
25. Nom Wah Tea Parlor — D2
26. Xi'an Famous Foods — D2
27. Kopitiam — D2
28. Fei Long Market Food Court — A1

JAPANESE

29. Mama Sushi — J5
30. Hasaki — E3
31. Kyo Ya — E3
32. Omen Azen — E2
33. Karasu — B3

PIZZA

34. Babbalucci — J5
35. Saraghina — B5
36. Ribalta — E2
37. Brooklyn Firefly — A1
38. Lucali's — B2
39. Stromboli Pizza — E3
40. Giuseppina's — A2

ITALIAN

41. Zero Otto Nove — J8
42. Bar Primi — E2
43. Via Carota — E2
44. I Sodi — E2
45. Hearth — E3

BURGERS

46. Burger Joint — G3
47. The Spotted Pig — E2
48. Shake Shack — F3
49. J.G. Melon — E2
50. Springbone — E2
51. Brindle Room — E3
52. Minetta Tavern — E2
53. Burger and Lobster — F2

LATIN

54. El Economico — J8
55. La Nueva España — J6
56. Los Tacos No. 1 — F2
57. Panca — E2
58. ATLA — E2

SOUTH ASIAN

59. Hanoi House — E3
60. Pye Boat — G6
61. Indochine — E2
62. Pongal — F3
63. Patel Brothers — F8
64. Kismat — J6

MUSEUM EATS

65. The Modern at the MoMA — G3
66. Untitled at the Whitney — F1
67. Flora Bar at the Met Breuer — H4
68. Cantor Roof Garden Bar at the Met — H4
69. Studio Café at the Whitney — F1
70. The Norm at Brooklyn Museum — A4

SPECIAL OCCASION

71. INSA — B3
72. Per Se — H3
73. Blue Hill — E2
74. Gallow Green — F2
75. Famous Sammy's Roumanian — D2
76. Strip House — G3
77. Sammy's Fish Box — J8

ICE CREAM

78. Milk Bar — E
79. Morgenstern's Finest Ice Cream — D
80. Snowdays — E
81. Van Leeuwen — D
82. L&B Spumoni Gardens — A
83. Sundaes and Cones — E

FOOD TRUCKS & PICNICS

84. Saigon Vietnamese Sandwich Deli — D
85. Sahadi 187 — E
86. Smorgasburg — E
87. Union Fare — E
88. Lobster Place — F

COCKTAILS

89. Irvington — E
90. Dead Rabbit Grocery and Grog — C
91. Hotel Delmano — D
92. The Ides at Wythe Hotel — D
93. Maison Premiere — D
94. Two E Bar — G
95. Salon de Ning — G
96. Grand Bar — D

HOT DRINKS

97. Café Colette — D
98. CHOCnyc — J
99. Abraço — E
100. Konditori — D
101. City of Saints — E
102. Té Company — E

GROCERIES & GIFTS

103. Roni-Sue's Chocolates — D
104. Eataly — F
105. D. Coluccio and Sons — A
106. PJ Wine — J
107. Zabar's — I3
108. Sahadi's — B
109. Fairway — H

GREENMARKETS

110. Union Square — E
111. Grand Army Plaza — A
112. Tucker Square — H
113. Fort Greene Park — B